Conversations with the New Testament

LEARNING CHURCH

Conversations with the New Testament

John Holdsworth

scm press

Published in 2014 by SCM Press

Editorial office
3rd Floor
Invicta House
108–114 Golden Lane
London
EC1Y 0TG

SCM Press is an imprint of Hymns Ancient & Modern Ltd
(a registered charity)
13A Hellesdon Park Road
Norwich NR6 5DR, UK

www.scmpress.co.uk

Biblical extracts are from the Revised English Bible © Oxford University
Press and Cambridge University Press 1961, 1970.

British Library Cataloguing in Publication data
A catalogue record for this book is available
from the British Library

978 0 334 04413 0

Typeset by Regent Typesetting
Printed and bound by
CPI Group (UK) Ltd, Croydon

Contents

Acknowledgements

This book is written in an innovative style and I am grateful to those who have persevered with my vision for it, and my commitment to a more experienced-based approach. In particular that means Professor Leslie Francis who has been an unfailing guide and encourager. I am grateful too to Bishop Michael Lewis and Canon Robert Jones for reading the script and assessing its suitability as a resource in their situations.

I find that the birth of a grandchild is a compelling prompt to start writing again, for many reasons. One of which is that it gives me the pleasure of dedicating the finished product.

To Evan John Holdsworth *gyda chariad*

Preface

How do you start a meaningful conversation about the New Testament? There are lots of books that make no pretence of *not* being a conversation. They are a lecture, a pitch, a presentation. They tell you what scholars have been doing over the past 200 years, but are not overly interested in what you are doing now. We all know people whose conversations are like that, and we have names like 'bores' to describe them.

Alongside that is a recognition that the New Testament begins by telling us, in Mark's Gospel, that it is to be a presentation of good news (the modern translation of the old English word 'gospel'). That seems to imply a two-way communication process. Good news is only good and news when it is recognized as such by people in an act of communication. Too often the Church's good news has actually sounded more like a set of slogans. Recently a teacher was telling me about a class he taught in a traditional way about the passion and crucifixion of Christ. People took notes dutifully. Later the same week there was a school outing to watch the film *ET*. Half the class was reduced to tears, and he was left wondering why people who were clearly moved by this piece of fiction were unmoved by the central New Testament message. It had ceased to be news. It had ceased to be good. It had ceased to be affecting.

What this book does is to start with current experience and ask: what does good news sound like to you? And having established that, to see whether a conversation is possible with the New Testament about something we actually care about. The book tells the story of some people who attend a church learning group that is set up to study the New Testament. You, the reader, are invited to step into that world and share that experience as it is mediated by Abi and Tim, Alice and others: to do the reading they do and to share in the exercises they attempt. The hope is that you too will find that a conversation is possible that uses your experience to shed light on New Testament texts and start a real piece of communication. Along the way, clearly there will be a need to explain how others have conversed too – to see something of the history of scholarship – and hopefully to see that scholarship is not just for bores but can be accessible and interesting for everyone.

John Holdsworth
April 2014

1

Starting a Conversation

Introduction

I want to introduce you to Abigail and Timothy. They are among the members of a new group, the initiative of churches in the area where they live, called a Learning Group. They are not sure what to expect, and are almost surprised to see themselves there. Tim has come because he was assured that this was not going to be something intense and emotional, but rather an enjoyable, stimulating experience that was about what its title suggested: learning. Tim had increasingly felt frustrated by his lack of knowledge. When he heard clever people criticizing Christianity in the media he didn't feel he knew enough to join in. When he heard hot gospellers delivering their message at full blast in the market square on Saturday mornings with full musical accompaniment, he felt embarrassed and frustrated. Was this really what Christianity was about? Was this the extent of its message? On the other hand, listening to the often glib use of jargon from the pulpit in his own church left him wondering what the so-called good news of Christianity really amounted to. He wanted to know more, and to get behind the jargon. He wanted to understand what intelligent people were saying about, for example, the Bible, which was to be the subject of the first sessions.

More specifically they were to be about the New Testament, and that appealed to Abi because she felt that was a point at which she might be able to access some new understanding. The New Testament was fairly familiar, or at least bits of it were. Her reasons for coming were a little different. She wanted not so much to know more, as to get more involved in some way. She went to her church, she would say regularly; the minister would say sporadically, but it all seemed to stop there. She felt this might be a time in her life to deepen her commitment but she wanted a reason for doing that. She wanted to be inspired, given a new perspective on life. She wanted to see if there was anything beyond the rather flat and predictable presentation of Christianity she'd grown to expect, and she thought that perhaps current scholarship on the New Testament might just provide that.

One other thing that appealed to her was that she did not feel she really knew all that many people who went to church. The after-church coffee group seemed to have developed a club mentality of its own that felt quite difficult to break into, and she was hoping she might meet a few new people with whom she would have something in common – namely the desire to know more about the Christianity they professed. Looking round the group, as they introduced themselves, she could see what a mixed group they were. She was going to have more in common with some than others, but she supposed that was what a group was all about. Some people seemed quite comfortable using religious language in a way that was not natural to her. One woman, Alice, did that but was obviously such a nice person that Abi felt she would give her the benefit of the doubt and see what she could learn from the way Alice saw things, and perhaps understand her better.

She was encouraged by the facilitator, Ken. He said that, so as not to waste anyone's time, this would not be a course for those who wanted to dig themselves further in to entrenched positions, whatever they might be. He said that this would be a time for exploring, and that exploring was a fascinating and exciting thing to do, and was often best done in a way that could let people share the experience. He said the group should not imagine that theology, the study of everything to do with faith and faith communities, was a matter of passing on timeless agreed truths, as if every member turned up with a sack and his job was to fill it with a shovel full of this and a shovel full of that, and then see if people could carry it away. He said they should not feel intimidated by the terms 'academic' or 'expert'. The content of what would be delivered was scholarly and up to date, but it was a starting point for the real business of theology, which was about interpreting our own lives, discipleship and situations in the light of what we learned, and so finding new truths from the way in which the ancient stories spoke to our experience.

He said that there had been something of a shift, in any case, in the scholarly study of the New Testament in recent years. There had been a move away from an approach that needed lots of scholarly input to tell us about life in the time of Jesus, or how ancient texts were passed on, or the exact meanings of ancient Greek words, though each of those areas was important in the bigger picture. There was much more emphasis now on the art of the different writers and the skills they employed to get their message across and persuade their readers.

Setting aims

There are some things I hope everyone will get out of this, he said. By the end of the course you should feel confident to work with passages from the New Testament. To achieve this we shall spend some time of every session with passages of text, and there will be exercises for everyone to join in that should be both challenging and fun, to show how we can approach the meaning of the text from different directions, but especially from the direction of our own experience. But this isn't all about us. We shall also introduce you to some of the ways scholarly critics have dealt with the text. We expect that you will gain a working knowledge of the contents of each of the books of the New Testament, and be aware of some of the main issues that have divided scholars in relation to them. Hopefully by the end of the course, you will be able to give an account of the current state of play on some of those questions, and perhaps even have an opinion of your own about them. Perhaps you will want to read more and explore further and so every session I will give out a sheet with some further suggestions about how to do that.

This reassured Tim who had been worried that the whole thing was sounding a bit airy-fairy. Ken continued: the traditional way to have a course like this, he said, has been to go through the books in turn, perhaps with a general introduction to different types of literature such as Gospels or Letters. But we're going to do something different. What I want us to get into, he said, is the mindset of those early Christian writers who felt they had something new to say that was good news to their hearers, and especially into the mindset of the hearers who actually experienced it as good news. We hear a lot of talk in churches about the gospel, as if it were some kind of constant commodity, and a lot of the time what preachers have to say is neither news nor particularly good.

Ken continued: So for our first activity, I want everyone to make a list of up to ten pieces of good news that they have heard, or would like to hear, or know someone who would like to hear. And, he said, just to set us off, my wife's pregnant at the moment, and the best news I hope to hear in a few months' time is, 'you've got a healthy baby, Mr Smith'. We all know what is good news for us – not the superficial stuff like winning the lottery, hoping Leeds United will get promotion or hoping we'll win a luxury cruise, but the kind of news that can really make a difference for the better to people or situations: news that can change things, because that's what those New Testament people believed. Both Abi and Tim, independently thought they might enjoy this and set about their lists.

TO DO

You might like to do the same as Abi and Tim: make a short list of the things that really mean good news to you.

Abi thought vaguely that hers looked like a list of prayers, and something in her brain was telling her that there was a connection, but she couldn't quite get there. For example, some were specifically about family members and friends who were ill or in a process of diagnosis. Others were about some of the world's intractable problems. These were the staple of prayers every week in her church, and she thought perhaps they were a bit predictable, so she included a piece of good news that was personal – after a year of struggling to start a new Internet business, it was still going strong. Then she thought about whether she ever brought good news to anyone else, and what that consisted of. How detailed and personal should she be? Just before she had come out, one of the children had woken up from a bad dream. Don't worry, Mummy's here, she had said. That was good news wasn't it, and not far removed from the kind of thing she sometimes said to people she visited in hospital. Don't be afraid. It's surely always good news to know you're not alone, and that you have friends, she thought.

Tim thought there must be an answer to the question that Ken was expecting, and he wanted to get it right. He had always been told that the Church's good news was about being saved from sin, and he wrote that down, and then crossed it out. It just wasn't him. It looked too holy there on the page. And anyway, the whole point of coming here was to move away from easily pronounced but hardly understood slogans. And yet there must be something in that. It got a mention every week somewhere in church, whatever it meant. He wrote it in again. Then he tried to unpack it a bit, wondering if he could put what he thought it meant into his own words. Good will always win out over evil, was his first attempt, and he quite liked that. If it was true it was good news and a great relief. Reading the papers, you began to doubt whether there was any purpose to life at all, and whether anybody or anything had any control over it all. He had been shocked by the most recent allegations about gang culture in the capital, and had begun to wonder if human society had ceased to be possible. It would certainly be good news to find that it was possible.

After a few minutes everyone gave Ken their lists. Both Abi and Tim were glad that, at this stage, they didn't have to read them out in public. However, they were relieved and pleased to find that there was quite a convergence of ideas, even though there were obviously different ways of phrasing things. Tim suspected that other people had something about being saved from sin without it being as awkward as it was for him, but he was prepared to accept that. Perhaps good news wasn't that difficult to define after all.

TO DO

How did your list compare with Abi's and Tim's?

Conclusion

Ken said that he could see eight general headings that could guide discussion over the coming weeks. Almost everyone put health and healing issues at the top of their list. That would be followed by the big question about whether life has meaning and if so what it is. Abi's idea about not being afraid and not being alone was chosen for the third session, and what seemed to follow from that was Tim's concern about society and community, and a further session about belonging and friendship. The traditional 'saved from our sins' agenda featured next. Let's see if we can give it some modern clothes, said Ken. That linked in with the tensions between good and evil. And finally Abi was surprised that Ken chose 'we're still in business', as the title of the final session. Because we are, he said. We're here and we still want to learn more. That's good news in itself.

Ken said that he hoped everyone had enjoyed the activity. There will be more of those every week, he said, and most of them will involve you reading bits of the Bible text, so be sure to bring a Bible along. At that point they moved on to the curry supper. If this is what church learning's about, bring it on, thought Tim.

2

The Scan Is Clear

Healing and good news

Ken started with this particular bit of good news, because it came high on virtually everyone's list. When we begin to think about what good news sounds like and what might be the best news we could hear, it's highly likely that getting positive news about our health will be high on the list. What can compare with the news that the treatment has been successful, the scan is clear, and we have been healed. Abi began to wonder which of the group had heard that particular bit of good news recently, and wondered if anyone would own up to it, but no one did. She reflected that often health matters are very personal indeed. Tim on the other hand, was uneasy that healing should just be thought about in personal terms. For him healing was a much wider idea. If he thought about all the areas where reconciliation and forgiveness were needed, for example, that took him to the realm of domestic and international politics as well as personal well-being, and he hoped that the session would include that dimension.

Ken put Tim's mind at rest by starting the session with an invitation to try and find other words for healing and list them. He was able to put forgiveness and reconciliation. Abi wrote down wholeness. Alice wrote atonement.

TO DO

What words would you use to 'flesh out' what 'healing' means for you?

Gospel healing passages

The next task was to look at some Bible passages that described healing, and to see, first of all, which of the terms the group had come up with seemed appropriate to each story. Because there were so many passages, Ken asked each member to read just one and describe it to the others, then to read a second passage that had appealed from the descriptions they had heard. Ken's list was as follows: Mark 2.1–12; Mark 5.1–20; Mark 5.22–24, 35–43; John 4.46–54; Matthew 20.29–34; Mark 6.45–52; Matthew 14.22–32; Luke 17.11–19; Matthew 8.28—9.1.

TO DO

Join in with the group's activity. Read as many of the passages above as you wish, or share what you've read. Look for the different kinds of healing you've identified and see if there is anything else that strikes you about the different accounts. Are there ways in which they differ from each other? Are there clues in the stories that suggest why the author thought they were important to include? What do you think he was trying to demonstrate – and is that the same in each case?

The same but different

The feedback session that followed was an eye-opener for both Tim and Abi, and it seemed to raise important questions for Alice as well. Tim had thought the initial question rather odd, but when he began reading the passages he began to see what Ken was getting at. He thought he would start with the passage from Luke. Reading this story about Jesus healing ten lepers, and only one Samaritan leper returning to give thanks, Tim could not help thinking that the healing was not the central point. Actually, Jesus did not perform any ritual of healing and did not touch the lepers. They were simply cleansed on their way to the priest, and the chief interest seemed to be that this happened in Samaria, and that the grateful man was a Samaritan, a hated foreigner as far as Jews were concerned. Meanwhile Abi had started with the Mark 2 passage. This seemed to be a story with three points. The first was that Jesus has the power to heal. The second was something about Jesus' power to forgive, and by extension about the link between illness and sin. The third was about the faith of the four friends who bring the paralysed man to Jesus in the first place. Next she read the passages at the end of Mark 5, which were also about faith in Jesus, and was surprised as she turned to John 4 that there were remarkable similarities between these two accounts and yet substantial differences.

Alice was also making this discovery. She had a Bible with lots of cross-references. She had noticed that Mark 5.1–20 was cross-referenced to one of the other passages, Matthew 8.28—9.1. A little bit of detective work saw her comparing Mark 6 with Matthew 14. Then she discovered that the incident in Matthew 20 was also found in Mark 10.46ff. and in Luke 18.35 ff. In the feedback session Alice was the first to speak. She said that obviously there would be differences between the Gospels, because the memories of the different apostles would vary slightly. Abi was not totally persuaded by this, particularly on the differences she had seen between Mark and John. After everyone had shared their questions and observations, Ken continued by asking if there could be such a thing as a typical Gospel healing account. They all had some things in common, but some of the differences clearly needed to be explained.

He said, we might note that there are very many similar-looking stories scattered throughout the Gospels: stories in which Jesus heals someone, gets a response, and in that context is able to make some kind of statement. We might want to call these stories 'miracles', but that is not a term that the Gospels themselves favour. In the first three Gospels, they are normally referred to (in the original Greek, despite some modern translations into English) as 'acts of power'. In John's Gospel, they are referred to as 'signs'. This is just one of the differences between John's Gospel and the other three. The 'signs' that John describes include only two or perhaps three of what the other Gospels call acts of power, but he does include six signs that are found only in the Fourth Gospel. That compares with eleven 'acts of power' that are repeated in the each of the other three Gospels.

Sources

Closer examination of all four Gospels shows that John is different from the other three in a number of respects. The style is different. There is no reference to some of the key moments in the other Gospels: for example, the transfiguration. There are no instances of Jesus telling the stories we call parables. In John there are a number of long speeches by Jesus (the passage from 14.27—16.16 is simply Jesus speaking without interruption). Even the order is slightly different. Jesus cleansing the Temple comes at the beginning of his ministry in John, but towards the end, just before the events that lead to the crucifixion of Jesus, in the other three Gospels. And it's not just that the first three are different from the fourth. It's also evident that the first three are similar to each other: in the order in which they place events, in the events they include, in the language they use, and in their common witness to parables and what we want to call miracles. This has been one starting point for the academic study of these texts using the tools of the historian. And the conclusion they reached is that the first three Gospels were put together using four sources.

As gently as possible, for Alice's benefit, Ken explained that from the outset it was clear to scholars that the exact verbal correspondence between large parts of the three Gospels ruled out any idea that the Gospels were similar because the authors' memories of events were the same. Any three people witnessing the same events might tell a recognizably similar story, but they would not use the exact same words. Only when there is some independent source does that happen. In this case then it is clear that two of the authors were using the work of the other as one of their sources. Which Gospel was first? Well, despite the order in our Bibles, the generally accepted view is that Mark was first. Mark's Gospel is 661 verses long, and of those, 600 occur in the much longer Gospel of Matthew. Most of the missing verses are incidental details. Mark also uses some technical non-Greek terms that the others avoid. It's easier to see why Matthew should have built on Mark, rather than that Mark shortened Matthew. Also Matthew and Luke never agree when they diverge from Mark, and crucially they follow his order. So we imagine a situation where Mark is first and Matthew and Luke both have a copy of Mark available to them when they write their Gospels.

TO DO

Read the following passages: Mark 6.30–34; Luke 9.12–17; Matthew 14.13–20 and John 6.1–15. These are four accounts of what we think of as the feeding of the five thousand, one of the few accounts to be in all four Gospels. Make a list of what the accounts have in common, and where they differ. For example, Mark's account is 14 verses long, but Luke's is only 5. What has been missed out? How similar are Matthew and Luke? How does John differ? (Look especially at the conclusion of each passage.) Does what you find illustrate the conclusions of scholars in any way?

The next thing that these so-called source critics noticed was that Matthew and Luke both included common material that was not in Mark, and that too seemed to have come from an independent source. An example would be the stories of the temptation of Jesus in the wilderness, which occur in almost identical form in Matthew and Luke but are absent from Mark. It looked like this could be a second source.

That still leaves some material unaccounted for. There are some well-known parts of each of the Gospels of Matthew and Luke that are peculiar to them. For example, their stories around the birth of Jesus are quite different. Matthew alone has the story of the sheep and the goats. Luke alone has the story of the good Samaritan, the prodigal son and Zaccheus. It looked as if each writer had access to material of his own. So the four sources are: Mark, the material common to Matthew and Luke which is not in Mark, material only in Matthew and material only in Luke. For convenience these four are normally referred to as Mark, Q, M and L.

Getting behind the jargon

Synoptic Gospels. *A collective term for the first three Gospels, which are so close that you can place them side by side in a so-called synopsis to examine their similarities. We shall use this term from now on.*
Source Criticism. *The name usually given to the process we have just described.*
Q. *Much of this early work (nineteenth century) was carried out by German scholars, so they chose the terminology in their own language. Q is the first letter of the German word,* Quelle, *which was the name given by scholars there to the source.*
Theology. *Used in our context to mean the particular bundle of ideas and beliefs about God, and especially Jesus, and their implications, that a particular early church community might have held in common.*

Eye-witnesses or modern authors?

Of course, once we move from the idea that here we have four eye-witness accounts from apostles who are trying to remember what they saw and heard (and getting it more or less together but slightly different) to the idea of writers using sources, everything changes. And when further study leads to the accepted conclusion that the first of these Gospels was not written (or perhaps more accurately, published) until the early 60s – some 30 years at least after the first Easter, new questions are raised and new insights emerge.

- The authors are seen in a new way, rather more like modern authors.
- Their own identity and biography becomes less important.
- There is a new interest in how and when the stories about Jesus (originally passed on by word of mouth) came to be written down.
- Why were the Gospels ever written, and why were they produced in the form that we have them?
- If there was such a big gap between the events and the writing, how historically reliable are these accounts? Can we depend upon them to hear the authentic voice of Jesus?

This was quite a lot for both Tim and Abi to take in. These were questions that had never really occurred to them, but they were fascinated and did not see them as a challenge to faith. After all, the scholars in question were mostly, if not all, people of faith themselves, who were trying to use their skills in the service of their faith. For Alice it was clearly more difficult, but the more she thought about it, the less challenging it became. The bottom line for her was that the gospel was the inspired word of God, and that could be true, however the traditions were passed on. In fact in some ways it made the whole thing even more remarkable, more miraculous. The most challenging conclusion was undoubtedly the last. Can we be sure that the Gospels record the authentic word of Jesus? Ken was quite reassuring on this point, though he did say that many scholars have degrees of doubt about the extent of the early Church's and early writers' own creative input.

> ## TO DO
>
> Which of the bulleted conclusions above do you find the most
> challenging? If challenging is not the right word for you, what
> word would you choose to describe your reaction to these
> conclusions?

Building blocks

The group learned that these questions had led to a large amount
of scholarly work in the twentieth century. This had the effect of
further dismantling the Synoptic Gospel accounts into small units,
alongside a renewed interest in what primitive Christianity was
actually like. What were its concerns? How was it doing theology?
What were the questions it grappled with? How was its mission
conducted? In working with their materials, how creative were the
Evangelists? And can we see evidence to answer those questions by
examining what look like the building blocks of the Gospels.

The basic technique used at this stage is again described and remembered primarily using German terms (see below). But in essence
it's a three-stage process. Stage one is to classify the material by
gathering together similar sorts of writing, so dividing the material
by genre. Miracle stories would be one example of a genre. Stage
two is to try and discover the original setting in real life in which
this particular kind of material might have been remembered and
passed on. For example, some kinds of material might have been
used in church worship and passed on in that way. Others might
have been part of the Church's sermons, or perhaps part of the
standard preparation of those who wanted to become Christians
through baptism. Perhaps some was part of the Church's mission
message as the Church expanded into other cultures. There are lots
of assumptions here, but scholars had fun trying to guess about
this. The final stage was to try and reach an assessment about how

historically reliable the particular kind of material might be or to devise tests to see which was the most reliable.

Getting behind the jargon

This whole process is called **Form Criticism,** *which is a straight translation from the German. The first stage uses the German word for genre,* **Gattung,** *the second stage uses the German for situation in real life,* **Sitz im Leben,** *and the convenient term for the third kind of enquiry uses the English word for historical-ness,* **historicity.**

So, with regard to the miracle stories for example, they are fairly easily identifiable and can be further subdivided into those that are concerned with healing and those that are concerned with nature. The situation in which they might have been preserved was that of mission to areas where divine beings only had credibility if they could perform miracles. Some scholars thought that due to their spectacular nature they might have spent more time in a secular rather than a church setting. That has implications for how historically reliable they might be. Alice felt she might have some difficulty coming to terms with the idea that what we are reading in the Gospels may actually be a presentation of Jesus and his significance as seen by the earliest Christian community, rather than a record of historical fact.

The big picture

By the latter half of the twentieth century scholars were tiring of looking at small portions of Synoptic Gospel material rather than the whole finished product. In the group Ken used the picture of building a wall to describe the next stage. Form critics, he said, were very good at identifying the bricks, knowing where they had come from and how old they were and what they looked like. But now the time had come to see what kind of wall each Gospel-writer built with the bricks they had. This is called *redaction criticism*. The conclusions from earlier scholarship with which they were working were:

- the Gospels are not eye-witness accounts, but rely on sources;
- there is a purpose to the way those sources are used. Gospels have an agenda;
- the Gospels are crafted creations produced in response to the needs of early Christian communities (such as in situations of religious conflict, teaching and preaching).

So, what is generally thought of as the final stage of Synoptic Gospel study, using the tools of historians, concentrated on the final version of each Gospel and examined how it differed from the others. In principle, this should allow scholars to discover the motivation and standpoint of each individual author. The process is seen quite easily by asking, for example, why Matthew changed Mark. Answering that question helps to show any consistent themes in each author, which can also be checked against Matthew's use of his own source M. The effect is to build an idea of the distinctive theology of each Gospel-writer. It does tend to put a final nail in the coffin of those who think that the Gospels could be source documents for a 'Life of Jesus'. Redaction criticism leads to the most sophisticated statement that what we have in the Gospels is interpretation and presentation, and not innocent fact. It also helps us to begin to appreciate the distinctive styles, priorities and arguments of each individual Gospel. Ken said that it is only by reading each of the Gospels carefully that we can begin to appreciate their differences and be fascinated by them. For example, anyone reading Luke, having engaged with this course, he said, would recognize that: it has a universal and inclusive feel; it places emphasis on prayer; it gives a much more important place to women; it seems to understand better how rich people think and act; and it has an awareness of the link between the life of Jesus and the Church.

On the other hand, anyone reading Matthew is: struck by the sense of imminent crisis; encouraged to feel that the law is a big issue; aware that relations between Jews and Christians is certainly

a priority; aware that Matthew is structured in a much more formal
way. It has collected together five blocks of teaching material and
has even been regarded as a teaching manual.

TO DO

A famous illustration of the work of redaction critics compares
the stilling of the storm in Mark and Matthew. Read Mark
4.35–41, then Matthew 8.18–27. The conclusion of the essay is
that whereas in Mark the aim is to demonstrate Jesus' power
over all that frightens us, in Matthew the aim is to steady the
nerve of the early Church as it faced difficulties. See if you
can find evidence for that yourself, then see if you can get hold
of a copy of the essay by G. Bornkamm. You might also compare Mark 6.45–52 and Matthew 14.22–32. Can you think of
reasons for the changes?

What redaction critics do is reach an interpretation of these changes
based on looking at the overall cumulative evidence of the whole
book. Mark is perhaps aware of Old Testament themes, and particularly how the Hebrew people were terrified of water. The people of
Israel were liberated after God had passed by, through the waters of
the Red Sea, and there are hints of and allusions to those themes. It
is also part of his purpose to present the disciples as uncomprehend-
ing. Matthew, on the other hand, likes to present the early Church
as being rather like a ship facing a rough time on a turbulent sea.
For Matthew, Peter represents church leadership, and in a kind of
'tough love' way, with Jesus berating the disciples for their lack of
faith, he seeks to inspire them to faith in turbulent times.

The next question is to ask why the authors wrote as they did.
What were the differences between different communities and
understandings that called for different emphases in different
Gospels? So in the end, this historical method brings us back to
historical questions, but it also leads to other approaches to the final
text, based on the methods used by literary scholars. And that too

is a huge and controversial shift, because, as we have noted, it takes the reader seriously in the quest for what the passage means and doesn't just rely on the conclusions of experts.

Gospels as literature

Ken said that the group was now about to enter a completely new phase of scholarship. He asked the group to think again about why different authors produced Gospels for their communities. Why did they need something new? Why were the existing Gospels not satisfactory? He asked them to think about faith communities they knew and to see if there is any common ground with the situation facing the first evangelists. Are all churches the same? Do they have different priorities? Does 'good news' have different priorities in different places?

TO DO

You might like to imagine what are important things that faith communities want to hear in settings like for example: a persecuted church, a church that has to live alongside another major world religion, a settled and rich church in a major western city.

Ken said that John 9 was a good place to begin to see how a more literary-critical approach might work. In this chapter, Jesus heals a man who has been blind from birth. All the action of the healing is described quite bluntly in the first seven verses of a chapter that is 41 verses long. The remainder of the chapter is taken up with the reactions of people who can't quite believe, or who don't want to believe what they see. First it's the neighbours, then it's the Pharisees. Later, the doubters are simply called 'the Jews'. Their interrogation of the man is aggressive, even brutal. He does not claim to know how his healing happened. His message is simply, 'I was blind and now I can see' (verse 25). As the story progresses, he himself grows in the realization that he should believe in Jesus, and as the climax of the story approaches he makes a confession of faith: 'Lord, I believe' (verse 38). This gives Jesus the opportunity to deliver the punchline: 'It is for judgement that I have come into this world – to give sight to the sightless and to make blind those who see' (verse 39).

What can we say about a passage like this from a literary scholarship point of view? The first thing is that we must be prepared to read it carefully, to look for clues as to the storyteller's art, and to see how the narrative and characters develop. If we read like this we see that the passage begins with Jesus repeating what he has just said in chapter 8: 'I am the light of the world.' That perhaps suggests that this chapter might add some flesh to that bald comment. Even before that, there has been a brief discussion about sin and illness. Each Gospel is keen to break the link in popular understanding between sin and disease. However, in some cases healing is closely connected with forgiveness and by implication the authority of Jesus to forgive sin. In this case, however, the healing is to demonstrate God working (literally). There is further reference to the fact that although it is now day (Jesus the light of the world is here at the moment), it will soon be night.

After these preliminaries, the man is healed, but now a whole series of scenes is presented in which everyone seems determined not to believe what they see (we might compare the later famous account of Thomas and the risen Christ, which occurs only in this Gospel). Alongside this we can also observe the growing realization of the man healed, of the significance of the healing. Literary scholars are keen to point out symbols in texts, and here the symbolism of light and darkness, day and night, sight and blindness are all played with to create what literary scholars would describe as irony. The people who are supposed to see are actually blind. They have the blindness of denial. This is a theme of the Gospel. The Prologue tells us that the tragedy that will unfold is traceable to the fact that the light of the world was in the world, but that people preferred darkness to light. However, the ultimate irony would be if we the reader did not see that the key point about this story is that the man was healed.

He was blind and now he can see. Jesus can heal every kind of blindness, and we are challenged to see what sort we might have.

Crossing boundaries

Ken now took the group back to Luke 17.11–19. Here Jesus heals ten people with the dreaded disease of leprosy, a disease that completed excluded them from the rest of human society. To be healed of leprosy was to be reintegrated and so, in a sense, to play a full part as a human being again. Luke emphasizes that this man was a Samaritan. Luke's is the most universal and boundary-crossing of the Gospels. Healing for him includes a boundary-crossing element (compare the story of the good Samaritan, also in Luke). This is not unconnected with forgiveness for, as our own experience shows, in a sense every act of forgiveness involves crossing a boundary. Tim reflected that when we think of healing in its political and world-wide sense today, we see the need for forgiveness in politics with the uncomfortable realities that former enemies have to work together if peace is to come and last.

This was not a concern in exactly those terms for Luke or those for whom he was writing, but it is a legitimate way of reading the text for us, and we might even claim a legitimate way of extracting its truth and meaning in our time. Literary ways of approaching texts do put great emphasis on the way that the texts contain truths that can be unlocked by different readers and perhaps different generations. This way of explaining things was helpful to Alice, who was beginning to wonder what Ken and the scholarly community of which he spoke actually meant by 'truth'.

Casting out demons

Then Ken came to the miracles to do with demons. These are more difficult for us to access, he said, and perhaps the most difficult of all is to be found in Mark 5.1–15. The story is also included in

Luke (8.27–39) where it has been slightly shortened, and Matthew (8.28—9.1) where it has been abbreviated even further, and changed so that two men are healed rather than one. This is the story of the demon-possessed man who is cured, and then in a spectacular sequel, the spirits that had inhabited the man were transferred to a herd of pigs who threw themselves into the sea. Matthew's treatment reflects his distaste for spectacular healing miracles. He often takes a story from Mark and, after giving a shortened and scaled down version, adds a kind of discussion – a little bit like the modern video package and studio discussion format we see on TV. Luke tells the story more or less in full, leaving out some of the more picturesque detail, but he does include what Matthew leaves out – the description of how happy this man was that he went around the region telling people about Jesus. This fits with Luke's agenda very well. This, after all, is Jesus' first trip abroad, and the man who is healed is the first foreign-based evangelist. Luke is keen to say that nationality does not matter. The issues here are universal. This man might want to say as his bottom line, echoing the blind man in John, 'Once I was mad. Now I am sane', and that feeling of joy transcends all boundaries. For Mark, it is a spectacular demonstration, and it follows other demonstrations of incomprehensible power showing domination of all that makes people afraid – whether that be hurricanes at sea or the mentally ill.

Conclusion

What Abi, Tim and the rest had learned in this session was that to begin to access the New Testament through the healing miracles is to be confronted by the different stages of New Testament scholarship over the past 200 years or so. It is thus possible to see how understanding and interpretation has moved on from regarding these miracles as factual accounts of what happened, to seeing them as useful media for presenting Jesus to a non-Jewish world, and within each Gospel a means of encapsulating some of the key theological interests of the Gospel. In the process we are brought to realize something about the variety of interpretations to be found even in the Gospels. Actually, they are not even all called Gospels. Mark's is. He invents the term. Matthew calls his work a book, and Luke an orderly account. We learn something about sources and the way they are used. We learn the importance of a close reading of the text. We learn to expect that the text is presented in a particular way to highlight some aspect of the author's agenda, and we are encouraged to expect that there is an agenda, and that we are being persuaded, however subtly, to buy into it.

But reading miracle stories introduces us also to some of the key themes of the New Testament and especially the Gospels. Those are themes about who Jesus really is and in what framework we can understand him; about forgiveness, reconciliation and the nature of society; about the Christian mission and to whom it should be directed, and about the common human emotions of joy, well-being and new hopefulness of those who know the scan is clear: who needed healing and, whatever the theology, have found it.

Conversations with the scholars

There are various categories of books you might consider. If you want an accessible dictionary/compendium with entries on a wide variety of subjects, then a very popular choice is: Green, McKnight and Marshall (1992), *Dictionary of Jesus and the Gospels.*

Critical introductions to the New Testament include: Wenham and Walton (2001), *Exploring the New Testament, Vol. 1, Introducing the Gospels and Acts*; Hooker (1979), *Studying the New Testament* (although this may seem dated, Morna Hooker is a giant of New Testament interpretation in the second half of the twentieth century, and this book was specifically written for people thinking about lay ministry); a classic exploration of the bigger picture of the New Testament world is Moule (1981), *The Birth of the New Testament* (3rd edn); for a more detailed and recent book with the same kind of remit you might try Burkett (2002), *An Introduction to the New Testament and the Origins of Christianity*; a recent general introduction is Boxall (2007), *SCM Studyguide: The Books of the New Testament*.

A good book for assessing the state of various critical questions about the New Testament in current scholarship is Powell (1999), *The New Testament Today*. If you are interested in particular critical approaches to the text, there is a series of useful essays in Barton (1998), *The Cambridge Companion to Biblical Interpretation*. Specifically on narrative criticism, a very accessible introduction is Powell (1993), *What is Narrative Criticism?*

Two good introductions to the miracles in particular are Richards (1975), *The Miracles of Jesus, What really Happened?* and John (2001), *The Meaning in the Miracles*.

Further reading

Barton, J. (ed.), 1998, *The Cambridge Companion to Biblical Interpretation*, Cambridge: Cambridge University Press.

Bornkamm, G., Barth, G. and Held, H. J., 1963, *Tradition and Interpretation in Matthew*, London: SCM Press.

Boxall, I., 2007, *SCM Studyguide: The Books of the New Testament*, London: SCM Press.

Burkett, D., 2002, *An Introduction to the New Testament and the Origins of Christianity*, Cambridge: Cambridge University Press.

Green, J. B., McKnight, S. and Marshall, I. H. (eds), 1992, *Dictionary of Jesus and the Gospels*, Leicester: InterVarsity Press.

Hooker, M. D., 1979, *Studying the New Testament*, London: Epworth Press.

John, J., 2001, *The Meaning in the Miracles*, Norwich: Canterbury Press.

Moule, C. F. D., 1981, *The Birth of the New Testament*, 3rd edn, London: A. and C. Black.

Powell, M. A., 1993, *What is Narrative Criticism?*, London: SPCK.

Powell, M. A. (ed.), 1999, *The New Testament Today*, Louisville, KY: Westminster John Knox Press.

Richards, H. J., 1975, *The Miracles of Jesus, What really Happened?*, London: Collins.

Wenham, D. and Walton, S., 2001, *Exploring the New Testament, Vol. 1, Introducing the Gospels and Acts*, London: SPCK.

3

In the End ... All Will Be Well

The bigger picture

Ken began the next session by saying how impressed he had been that all the good news suggestions that people had written down had not been narrowly self-centred. There was a real sense, he said, that people wanted to be reassured that life has meaning and purpose, and that it has morality and justice. Tim was pleased to hear this. 'There is a purpose to life' had been on his list, along with what could be called similar themes like 'there is someone in control of this chaos' and 'the good guy wins'. He had thought this might be a male-oriented choice, but clearly some of the women warmed to it too. Abi, whose neighbour had a son in the army, had put, 'the war is over', which she thought was in the same area. Alice had put, 'the devil and all his works are defeated', which Ken had translated into more everyday language as something to do with the end of evil.

TO DO

What do you think are the main challenges from your experience to the idea that life does have meaning? What are the things that make you despair about the world and its direction? If you were God, what things would you start putting right? Is it good news for you that life has meaning?

For Ken it was good news that life has meaning. This is not just a random and purposeless existence without significance in which human beings live for a short while, as petals on a flower, and then disappear without note or memorial, he said. We want to believe things like: our life counts, we are known, and in some way or other there is justice in creation. There's a line from a hymn that sums it up for me, he said: 'earth its destiny shall find'. And in a very important sense, that is what the New Testament is all about.

Ken now asked the group to test what he had just said, for themselves. Look at each of the four Gospels, he said, and write down what you think is the first piece of good news that Jesus is recorded as delivering.

TO DO

Join Abi and the others in their search of the four Gospels.

Both Tim and Abi came up with Matthew 4.17, though others had taken Old Testament quotations from chapter 3. In Mark everyone had got the parallel text, Mark 1.15 – 'The time has arrived; the kingdom of God is upon you. Repent and believe the Gospel', though some missed out the second sentence on the grounds that it was not in itself good news. Luke proved a little more puzzling. There was no early mention of the Kingdom here, but rather a quotation from the Old Testament about bringing good news to the poor at 4.18f. Tim wondered if the two verses there perhaps spelled out in ordinary terms what 'the Kingdom' meant, because if he was honest he was not sure. John was a challenge for everyone. Some had 1.51, though it seemed to make little sense. Some had 2.19, but was it good news? Alice thought 3.7, 'you must all be born again', was a piece of good news, but secretly Tim did not. He was quite happy being born just once. John 3.16 was one familiar-sounding saying that they could all agree on, even if they were not sure what was meant by eternal life.

The role of the Old Testament

In fact, said Ken, all those passages rely to some extent on understanding something about the Old Testament. Abi's heart sank. The Old Testament was a closed and daunting book to her. But Ken said it was really necessary. He said, it is quite futile to think we can read the New Testament as if the Old Testament did not exist and has no part to play in our understanding. He asked the group, just to prove the point, to find how many references to the Old Testament of one kind or another they could find in Matthew 2 and Luke 2. They were all surprised at how many they came up with, and in passing they noted that most of Matthew 1 and a big chunk of Luke 3 were taken up with family trees that connected Jesus right from the start with the Old Testament.

TO DO

You might look at Matthew 2 and Luke 2 as well, and notice the different ways that Luke and Matthew use their references to the Old Testament. Matthew quotes proof texts in a quite clumsy way. Luke is much more subtle, using the power of allusion. Compare, for example, Luke 1.46–55 with 1 Samuel 2.1–10. Why do you think the similarities might exist? What is Luke trying to say?

So Ken began. Within the Old Testament there is a great surge of theological creativity that accompanies the realization that there is just one God. Israel always believed that their God was the best god, but it was only after the events that we call the exile that they came really to consider what it meant to believe in one God. One result was the belief that if there is only one God then this must be the God of all creation, and so the designer not just of the static world, but also the designer of history and all that makes for political and social life as well. These beliefs were emerging just at a time when serious questions were being asked about suffering, and especially undeserved suffering. If God had created the world as God wanted it, why was there suffering. If God had designed history, why did there have to be war, violence and bloodshed. Why could there not just be peace and justice?

One group of writings that came to prominence in the consideration of these issues was what we now call apocalyptic writings. Between about 200 BC and AD 150 they were arguably the most important religious writings at the popular level. This was a time when questions about undeserved suffering and about God's plans for the people of Israel were particularly acute. They were an occupied and weak people, sometimes resorting to terrorist activity in a fight to preserve what was left of their national and cultural identity. How could that square with a God who had designed things? The apocalyptic writers' answer was to write as if they had a special revelation from God (literally an apocalypse) showing them how history was going to develop. They wrote as if time could be divided into different ages, and their usual standpoint was to write as if the end of one age was imminent and the next age about to begin. All that was wrong with the world was part of the passing age. All would be transformed in the next age when things would be made right and God's will would be given effect.

TO DO

The group was asked to look at some passages from the Old Testament and you might like to do the same. What do you think, on the basis of these writings, religious people hoped for? This is the list: Isaiah 9.2–7; Isaiah 11.1–11; Isaiah 25.6–9; Isaiah 60.1–3; Isaiah 61.1–3; Jeremiah 31.10–17; Jeremiah 31.29–34.

Abi thought there was a lot about gathering people together, and she noticed that quite a few of the things she was reading had been quoted in the first chapters of Matthew and Luke that she had read before. That must mean something. Tim also noticed that and words that stood out for him were *new covenant, forgiveness, justice and judgement.* He also noticed that there was quite a lot about food and celebrating with meals. Alice noticed references to the Messiah, the anointed one of God who would make things change.

Looking for change

Ken summed it up like this: from these readings and many others it was clear that there was need for threefold change. Human hearts must change. That would only be accomplished by a new emphasis on forgiveness. Human society must change. The changes were described in language that looked back to the ideal age of King David. So there was a hope for a new Kingdom of God, inaugurated by someone anointed as King as David had been (that is, in Hebrew a Messiah, or in Greek, a Christ). And finally the whole creation must change, so that there was no more danger in the world, no more suffering and tears and no more death. All of these changes would be inaugurated in what was described as a resurrection and would be accompanied by celebratory meals.

He went on. It was these hopes, expressed in this kind of language, that formed the discourse of religion during the 200 years before Jesus' ministry and were current at the time of it. The questions on everyone's lips were about the Kingdom of God, the resurrection, the Messiah or the Coming One, in the hope that one day there would be real evidence to give substance to the belief that earth had a destiny, that life had meaning and that God was central to it all. We can see evidence that these were popular themes at, for example, John 4.25, where an ordinary woman at the well acknowledges her understanding of the Messiah. It is almost quaintly authentic. 'I know that Messiah (that is, Christ) is coming,' she says. 'When he comes he will make everything clear to us.'

As a break from his voice, Ken asked the group to look at John 11.24. Here another ordinary woman, Martha, speaks about resurrection. Jesus is talking to her about her dead brother, Lazarus, and tells her that he will rise again. She says, 'I know that he will rise again at the resurrection on the last day.' Jesus goes on to say, 'I am the resurrection.' In the Synoptic Gospels the issue of whether Jesus is the one who is to come, or whether people should look for another, is a fairly constant theme. We see it, for example, at Matthew 11.3, where the disciples of John come with just that question. The evidence that Jesus gives is that the blind see, the lame walk, lepers are made clean, the deaf hear, the dead are raised to life, the poor are brought good news. All of these are the signs by which Christians want the Kingdom to be recognized (remember Luke 4.18f. and Isaiah 61.1). And they do recognize them in Jesus. The good news is not just that people are being healed, but that the healing itself provides the evidence that Earth has a destiny and life does have meaning, God is acting and the Messiah has arrived. The Kingdom is at hand.

TO DO

Throughout all the Gospels there is a constant sense of tension as Jesus is being tested against criteria that people believed would give them sure knowledge that the new age was about to dawn. Look again at the temptation accounts in Luke and Matthew (Luke 4.1–13; Matthew 4.1–11). Read them as if they were examples of popular testing to see if Jesus really were the Messiah. Read this way, what would they tell you about what people had come to expect and what was new and distinctive about Jesus' ministry? Compare this with Matthew 27.42.

Calling Jesus names

> **TO DO**
>
> Ken asked the group to do something in which you can share. Just look through one of the Gospels, Matthew for instance, and see how many different names and terms you can find for Jesus. Just for fun: how many do you think there will be? Abi thought about four, which she could think of without looking them up. Tim thought six. In fact there are at least 13 different names or designations for Jesus in Matthew's Gospel alone. See if you can find any you have missed.

Jesus is consistently described as Messiah or Christ or even on occasion son of David. His preaching and teaching is described as being about the Kingdom from the very beginning. Mark's first report of his message, as we have seen, is, 'The time has arrived; the kingdom of God is upon you. Repent, and believe the good news' (Mark 1.14). In Jesus' practical ministry Gospel-writers describe his actions as demonstrations of the new rules and ethos of the Kingdom in which the first will be last and the least greatest. He makes forgiveness the central hallmark of that ministry and calls for personal repentance. And at the end, Gospel-writers have such a sense of the importance of the events of the first Easter that they feel justified in using the term resurrection to describe them. The new age has dawned and Jesus has somehow ushered it in.

Other New Testament writers are equally aware of this theme of destiny and the new world order. In 1 Corinthians 15 Paul emphasizes the importance of the resurrection. For him as for the other New Testament writers this is a technical term with many connotations. Paul is not simply describing an event: he makes no mention of empty tombs or other historical details. For him the scale is bigger than that: 'Christ was raised to life – the first fruits of the harvest of the dead. For since it was a man who brought death into the world, a man also brought resurrection of the dead. As in Adam all die, so in Christ all will be brought to life' (1 Corinthians 15.20–22). The link between resurrection and a new creation is one that Paul uses elsewhere, often in connection with baptism. In Romans 6, for example, he says explicitly that through baptism we die and rise with Christ. 'By baptism into his death we were buried with him, in order that, as Christ was raised from the dead by the glorious power of the Father, so also we might set out on a new life' (Romans 6.4). In the climax to his letter to the Galatians Paul says, 'the only thing that counts is new creation' (6.15), and his own beliefs about the world's destiny are shaped by his conviction that Christ is the first fruits of a new creation himself. Death itself is seen as conquered (1 Corinthians 15.55) as a new life-bringing creation begins to take its place, accomplished by a second Adam.

Getting behind the jargon

This area of what we might call destiny studies is usually known by a term that derives from one of the Greek words for 'end' – **eschatology**. *Unfortunately this is sometimes translated to mean 'last things' and relegated to a siding inhabited only by those who have a particular interest in what happens after we die, or when supposedly the world ends (which according to a news item I've just been listening to should have been yesterday). Similar popular misconceptions accompany the term* **apocalyptic**. *This comes from a Greek word meaning 'that which is revealed' and apocalyptic writings get their name on that basis. Most scholars would regard these writings not as organs of doom and gloom, but as trying to convey a message of hope to beleaguered people. A final ambiguous term which is important is the Greek word* **parousia**. *This is a technical term whose exact meaning we cannot be certain about. The straightforward meaning is simply 'coming', but the situation is complicated, because this is the word used in a key Old Testament passage (Daniel 7.13) to describe the final vindication of those suffering or persecuted people who have kept faith in difficult times. This, in itself, is a sign of the beginnings of the celebrations of the new age. The picture in Daniel tells us that the vindication will happen as the people experience* a 'coming' (parousia) to one called the Ancient of Days. Some commentators, both ancient and modern, appear to have turned this on its head and spoken of 'a second coming of Christ' as the true meaning of parousia. The text itself was obviously in common usage. We see it quoted verbatim in the Gospels (for example Mark 14.62 (see below)), and it is alluded to in Stephen's vision as he is being martyred (Acts 7.56). For more discussion see below.

Returning soon?

During the mid years of the twentieth century there was a great deal of interest in eschatology generally and apocalyptic in particular, perhaps deriving from the horrendous experiences people had had during two world wars and a holocaust. Tim noted in passing that so much of what was creative in Christian thinking generally seemed to have come from times when people were suffering.

Of particular interest to scholars in the 1950s and 1960s was the time frame with which the New Testament was working with regard to the Kingdom. Is it the case that the Kingdom was still to come, near but not yet here. That would accord with human experience of all that is currently wrong with the world. Or is it the case that Jesus had declared the Kingdom already present. Those who held this view spoke of 'realized eschatology'. Or was it that Jesus had, as it were, fired the starting pistol, but the implications were still being worked out and not yet fully realized, even though they had been begun. This position is called proleptic or inaugurated eschatology. Good arguments can be made for each, but another important factor (as we have seen) needs to be taken into account. Different New Testament writers may hold different views on this issue. By common consent, for example, John presents the most realized eschatology in the New Testament. In his Gospel all has been revealed. There is nothing left to wait for.

There have been arguments that the early Church expected that Jesus would return to earth very soon, and also that his failure to do so resulted in the particular shape of some writings. In other words, the fact that what was expected did not happen created a crisis of belief. The Gospel of Matthew is sometimes cited as one that has this imminent expectation. The argument runs like this. The Church for Matthew is a short-lived expedient and the ethics he sets out are meant only to be in force for a short time – for the interim between the present and the second coming. The whole Gospel is imbued with a sense of crisis and with the need to make an urgent choice because the time is short. Other writers (such as Luke) are seen as setting out a view that the Church is going to be a long-lived institution, and so he presents little evidence of the expectation of an imminent return.

At this point, the group was asked what the term 'second coming' meant to them and how important an element of their faith it was. Alice went first and said that it was essential and one of the main-stays of her faith. Someone who rarely spoke said that if he had to believe like that he couldn't be a Christian. Both Abi and Tim might have said that they did not really think that much about it, but if they did, they certainly did not expect Jesus to return to earth riding on a cloud or something like that.

TO DO

What does the term 'second coming' mean to you? Whereabouts on the spectrum would you be, and does the kind of scholarship we are talking about here change your mind in any way?

Ken said it is notable that the term 'Kingdom' is hardly used out-side the Synoptic Gospels (for example Galatians 5.21), but in those Gospels it has a central place, though absent from John, where the term 'eternal life' has more coinage as the nub of the Christian message. The underlying assumption is that the Kingdom is present in the person of Jesus, but that teaching is needed about the King-dom because it is commonly misunderstood. Writings between the Testaments had sometimes given the Kingdom a very nationalistic or political or violent character. Jesus has to recover the concept.

One of the key places where we see teaching about the Kingdom of God is in the parables of Jesus, his favourite teaching medium.

Parables of the Kingdom

Parables are found in all four of the Synoptic sources. The parable of the sower would be an example of a parable from the Mark source (Mark 4.3–9). From the Q source we might choose the parable of the lost sheep (Matthew 18.12–14; Luke 15.1–7). We can see the different uses to which this parable has been put by each author. In Matthew it forms part of a collection of teachings about the import- ance of the least and is an example of how even one lost sheep is important. In Luke it is part of a collection about things that are lost and found, and so the emphasis is on the joy of rediscovery. Also from that chapter, and maintaining that theme, from the spe- cial L material we have the parable of the lost or prodigal son. An example from the M material would be the labourers in the vine- yard (Matthew 20.1–16). This is a classic Kingdom story about how Kingdom values are at odds with worldly values. When men are hired, their expectation is that those who are hired first and work longest will be paid most. Those hired last will be paid least. But in fact all are paid the same. When you consider that it is likely that the fit and strong are hired first and the weak and sickly last, the story is even more telling and challenging.

TO DO

Do you have a favourite parable? Find it and read it. What does it tell you about the Kingdom that either fits with or challenges the assumptions we've heard about so far?

Until the nineteenth century it was common to regard the parables as allegories. Classic work in the twentieth century reached new conclusions. Parables are not extended metaphors. They have just one point, and the primary focus of all of them is the Kingdom. They may begin with a question but commonly end with a challenge. They are thought to have authentic origins in the words of Jesus himself, though sometimes they have been 'doctored' by the early Church and sometimes the Church has clearly added an 'explanation' that makes them seem like extended metaphors. A good example would be the parable of the sower (Mark 4.3–9) with the church interpretation (4.13–20). It is from this teaching that the values of the new age become clear.

Getting behind the jargon

Alongside eschatology, one of the other key theological categories is **Christology**. *This is the study of the way in which the New Testament or any part of it presents Jesus. As we might say today: how do they package him? Clearly any such packaging has to begin with some sort of conversation with popular culture. If Jesus is to be presented in terms people understand, then the writers have to know what those terms are. We have already seen that Old Testament eschatology gives us some terms and ideas. In particular it gives us titles like Son of David, Messiah and Christ that can be used in the packaging. Christology commonly takes these so-called* **christological titles** *and explores how they are used so as to discover if they are related to particular theological standpoints or geographical areas, for example. So, Messiah, Rabbi or Son of David would have obvious resonance with a Jewish audience. For a Gentile audience, terms like Lord and Saviour might speak more directly.*

The title Son of Man is important for two reasons. First, it is the title of choice in some eschatological contexts. So in Daniel 7.13, which was obviously important in Jesus' time – it's quoted in several places as we have seen – it is the Son of Man who brings the faithful to the Ancient of Days to be vindicated. More than Messiah or Christ, this is the title that speaks of one who is at the threshold of a new age and is the agent of destiny. And that leads to the second point of importance: it is the only title that is ever placed on Jesus' lips in the Gospels. To put it bluntly, it's what Jesus is seen to call himself. (Note the careful choice of words here. It may be that this is a device on the part of the authors, but of course it may also be authentic.)

In the end

There are two places in the New Testament where we are made very aware of eschatological and apocalyptic themes. One is a portion of each of the Synoptic Gospels (Mark 13; Matthew 24; Luke 21) in which Jesus is cast as a prophet, foretelling what will happen soon. This so-called 'Little Apocalypse' has its most heightened form in Matthew, which is in any case more fond than the others of apocalyptic style. It is always important to remember that this form of writing derives from contexts where people are suffering and can see little evidence of God's concern or presence. Writers are at pains to defend God, to cast God as engaged in a battle (often) against evil that brings huge collateral damage. The important thing for the community is that they remain pure, faithful and free from idolatry. In the end the Son of Man will vindicate them at his parousia. These sections are thought to be late additions to the Gospels and may come from a background of persecution of Christians by Jews in the early years (cf. John 16.1–4, 21–24, 32–33).

The other example is the book of Revelation itself, sometimes called 'The Apocalypse'. This book, too, may well be directed to people who are being persecuted, either in some state programme or, more likely, in local vigilante-style hits. The theme once again is God's victory over evil, the need to maintain faith in the face of all the evidence that such faith is worthless and the need to remain pure. The book is directed to seven particular churches, though that may be a literary device. Each church is assessed and reviewed before the 'vision' itself. The whole is redolent with overtones of the Church's liturgy and concentrated references to the Old Testament and other favourite apocalyptic sources. Tim was disappointed to learn that revelation, the Apocalypse, is not about the destruction of the world in some terrible way. That was certainly how he had understood the term from the way it was used in film titles or news-paper reports about global warming. Still, it was reassuring to know that the underlying theme was that God was in fact in control and that in the end all will be well.

Conclusion

Summing up, Ken said that thinking about this particular kind of good news brings us into contact with key New Testament themes and areas of scholarship. It reminds us of important New Testament words and ideas, like Kingdom, and turns our attention to the big picture of what Christianity is actually about. In the process we are introduced to the concepts of eschatology and Christology, and we see one way in which a connection is made between the Old Testament and the New. We understand the important and particular role of parables and, building on last session's insights, see how eschatological traditions and literary genres can play a part in building individual theologies.

Tim was beginning to think how much he liked the course, and just how much he had learned in the last two sessions. It reminded him uncomfortably of what he had taken for granted over many years. Alice was happy as long as they spent substantial time reading the Bible itself, and Abi could agree in the end with the reassurance that the texts on this subject brought, if for different reasons.

Conversations with the scholars

Some of the books already mentioned will be useful. Neither eschatology nor Christology are popular subjects for systematic treatment in their own right at the moment. The classic such treatments of both subjects date back around 40 years or so. Authors now are more inclined to be less systematic and to deal with these subjects within commentaries or other works specifically related to particular New Testament texts. Two good introductions to the world of eschatology and end-expectation are Gowan (2000), *Eschatology in the Old Testament* and Russell (1992), *Divine Disclosure*. A classic systematic treatment of Christology is Fuller (1969), *The Foundations of New Testament Christology*. An interesting introduction to some of its issues is presented by Richards (1973), *The First Christmas: What Really Happened?*

Specifically on the parables of the Kingdom, the classic treatment is Dodd (1961), *The Parables of the Kingdom*. A more recent assessment of the state of this study is Gowler (2000), *What Are They Saying about the Parables?*

On the Kingdom of God, a classic treatment is Perrin (1963), *The Kingdom of God in the Teaching of Jesus*. A more recent summary of some of the issues raised there is Burkett (1999), *The Son of Man Debate: A History and Evaluation*.

On parousia, the issues are well rehearsed in a classic book, Robinson (1957), *Jesus and His Coming*. A bridge between the older systematic approaches and the newer more focused approaches is provided by a classic set of essays prompted by the rise of redaction criticism, for which it is also a very useful guide: Bornkamm, Barth and Held (1963), *Tradition and Interpretation in Matthew*.

Further reading

Bornkamm, G., Barth, G. and Held, H. J., 1963, *Tradition and Interpretation in Matthew*, London: SCM Press.

Burkett, D., 1999, *The Son of Man Debate: A History and Evaluation*, Cambridge: Cambridge University Press.

Dodd, C. H., 1961, *The Parables of the Kingdom*, rev. edn, London: Collins.

Fuller, R. H., 1969, *The Foundations of New Testament Christology*, London: Collins

Gowan, D. E., 2000, *Eschatology in the Old Testament*, 2nd edn, Edinburgh: T. & T. Clark.

Gowler, D. B., 2000, *What Are They Saying about the Parables?*, New York: Paulist Press.

Perrin, N., 1963, *The Kingdom of God in the Teaching of Jesus*, London: SCM Press.

Richards, H. J., 1973, *The First Christmas: What Really Happened?*, London: Collins.

Robinson, J. A. T., 1957, *Jesus and His Coming*, London: SCM Press.

Russell, D. S., 1992, *Divine Disclosure*, London: SCM Press.

4

No Fear

Taking stock

At the beginning of the next session, Ken invited everyone to share what so far they had found either really new and interesting or really new and challenging. Everyone was asked to think and write for a few moments before speaking. For Tim, it had come as quite a shock to start thinking about the Gospel-writers as if they were modern authors, weighing sources, presenting arguments, attempting both to inform and persuade. Abi had realized just how superficial her listening had been during all her years of attending church services. Suddenly she was being asked to appreciate nuances, look for irony, character development and follow a plot, in the same way that she had experienced in a reading club that she used to be part of. For Alice there were a number of challenges. She somehow had to reconcile what seemed like a very human process, discovered by very human scholarship, with the idea that the Scriptures are divinely inspired. While she could appreciate the integrity of historical-based methods of enquiry, she was less sure about treating the Bible like other literature. That challenged her idea of truth. But she was sticking with it. After all, the other people did take her concerns seriously, and they all showed some measure of commitment to what she thought was important. 'We are pilgrims on a journey,' she thought, echoing the sentiments of a favourite hymn.

TO DO

This might be a good time for you also to think about what has
been an exciting discovery and what has been most challenging
in the course so far. Make a list and see if any of your group
agree with Abi, Tim and Alice.

Ken said that much of this session's work would be consolidation.
From the group's original list of experienced good news, he had
chosen (what in fact Abi had written) some gentle words that everyone would recognize: 'it's all right, I'm here, don't be afraid'. He said
this might seem a bit of a quirky session, because it would group
together a number of New Testament features that were normally
treated in a different way, but he hoped that in the end it might
both hang together and be more memorable. He wanted to start
with the term 'gospel' as used by Mark.

Old Testament gospel

The fact that Mark called his work a Gospel, and that this was rightly
hailed a new genre of literature – there had never been anything
quite like the finished work before – did not mean that there had
been no concept of God's good news before the New Testament.
In fact, the word 'gospel' first appears in the tradition in the Old
Testament in the prophet Isaiah. The good news that Isaiah has in
mind is that Israel will be freed from the captivity of the exile and
able to return to their homeland. But arguably this definition of Old
Testament good news is too narrow. Perhaps a more appropriate
and earlier place to look is in those prophecies of hope that sustained Israel as they entered exile that are to be found for example
at Jeremiah 30.10: 'But do not be afraid, Jacob my servant; Israel, do
not despair, says the LORD' and verse 11, 'For I am with you to save
you, says the LORD.' In fact, these two ideas, that God will be with
his people, and that as a consequence they need not and should

not be afraid, form the basis of all subsequent Old Testament good news or gospel.

TO DO

Pause and think of times when you have been afraid, and of what brought you comfort. What does adult good news to the fearful sound like?

Ken said that the original peg for the session was obviously the kind of thing a mother might say to a child having a bad dream, but that the underlying sentiment was one that applied to many more adult situations. We recognize that life is not usually smooth, that there will be times of trial, sadness and perhaps even suffering, and the more mature forms of Christian faith accept that that is so and that God does not capriciously inflict suffering on people. What does bring consolation, though, is the belief that God is with us, shares our human concerns, understanding our condition, since he was himself born in human form. And even today that sense of God's presence has the power to dispel fear. We can still receive it as good news. In terms of a straightforward statement, it is the message of the angel to the shepherds at Jesus' birth in Luke's account: 'Do not be afraid; I bring you good news' (2.10). In Matthew's Gospel the same message is conveyed in the name 'Emmanuel', meaning God (is) with us. This message is repeated at the end of that Gospel: 'I will be with you always, to the end of the age' (28.20). In Mark's Gospel, when Jesus appears to the disciples walking on the water, his first words, seeing their terror, are, 'Take heart: it is I. Do not be afraid' (6.50).

The most obvious statement of the presence of God as good news is the incarnation itself. The witness of the New Testament is that Jesus is not just another prophet but that he is God. This is partly conveyed, as we have seen, through the use of christological titles. In the Synoptic Gospels these are the clues through which Jesus is packaged and presented. The suspicion that Jesus might be more than a prophet is then confirmed by his miracles, by the authority of his teaching, by the declarations at his baptism and transfiguration and finally by his passion and crucifixion. Mark has the centurion at the cross declare, 'This man must have been a son of God' (15.39), a sentiment echoed by Matthew (27.54). The titles chosen are dictated, when speaking to Jews, by the expectations set from Old Testament study or, when speaking to Gentiles, by the demands of starting a conversation with those from a different culture, idiom and background, in the context of missionary expansion.

Jesus in John's Gospel

But today, said Ken, I want us to look in a little more detail at the way in which Jesus is presented and packaged by John, because in the Fourth Gospel Christology is conveyed in a different way. A number of 'signs' point to who Jesus is for those who can recognize them for what they are. Each is numbered, beginning with the events at the wedding in Cana where Jesus turns water into wine. The Fourth Gospel states its purpose in John 20.31: 'Those (signs) written here have been recorded in order that you may believe that Jesus is the Christ, the Son of God, and that through this faith you may have life by his name.' In this Gospel, the 'packaging' of Jesus takes quite a modern turn as he appears in a number of what we might nowadays call photo opportunities. In the first part of the Gospel, prior to the start of the passion story proper, many of Jesus' significant sayings are set at a Jewish feast or religious festival and have that as their backcloth. These festivals each have their own significant symbols of God's presence and, in a succession of sayings that begin with the words 'I am ...', Jesus is seen to claim that he is the reality to which these symbols point. The sayings continue into the passion narrative itself.

> ## TO DO
>
> The sayings are sometimes called *ego eimi* sayings because those are the words in Greek that introduce them. This is a very emphatic way of speaking in Greek, meaning, 'I most certainly am'. The first significant one is to be found at John 6.35 (I most certainly am the bread of life.). See how many others you can find between there and what may be the last of the sequence at John 15.1.

The complete list of *ego eimi* sayings is as follows:

- the bread of life (6.35);
- the light of the world (8.12; 9.5);
- the door of the sheepfold (10.7);
- the good shepherd (10.14);
- the resurrection and the life (11.25);
- the way, the truth and the life (14.6);
- the true vine (15.1).

As to why this particular form of speech is so important in John's Gospel, there are various possibilities, many connected to the culture that different commentators believe is being addressed in the Gospel. But least controversially and most obviously, these sayings connect to the Old Testament and particularly to the name of God as disclosed in Exodus 3.14: 'I AM WHAT I AM' (and I shall be what I shall be), which is the translation of the Hebrew YHWH.

In the Fourth Gospel Jesus refers often to the Father's name. He comes in the name of the Father (5.43) and does his works in the Father's name (10.25). In 17.6, in his 'report back to the Father', Jesus says, 'I have made your name known to the men you gave me out of the world', and in verse 11 he prays, 'Protect them by the power of your name.' Being 'in the name' as Jesus is in the name is a means of identification between God and Jesus, and between God and humankind. This is a way of saying that God is in Christ. Study of this kind shows continuity between the Old Testament and the ministry of Jesus such that it builds confidence about God's presence, interest and protection in a way that gives substance to the command, 'Do not be afraid for I am with you.' Also, just as we have seen how eschatology operates as a theological discipline, looking at the 'I am' sayings gives us a further insight into what Christology is about and how it is undertaken.

Who Jesus is

It is not only through the use of christological titles, or through narratives setting out convincing evidence of God in action, as Jesus heals, teaches and performs miracles, that the authors of the Gospels seek to persuade us that Jesus is God-with-us. The literary style and skill of the authors, their use of vocabulary and symbol, can also be suggestive. In John's Gospel, for example, the author is particularly fond of using the word group that gives us the translation 'glory'. He uses this 41 times, compared to Matthew (11) and Mark (4). From an original meaning of something like 'reputation', the Old Testament uses the word glory to describe the physical effect of an unseen God. In the Old Testament this is often combined with the symbol of light. God's glory is portrayed as a kind of radiance. For the Synoptic Gospel-writers, the glory of Christ is essentially something that will be seen in the future – it is part of the eschatological package; but for John it accompanies Christ in the present. The Prologue tells us, 'We have beheld his glory' (John 1.14). Jesus shows his glory – his oneness with God – in the signs he performs and especially in his death (7.39; 12.16; 13.31). John combines this use of glory with a special interest in the symbolism of light (again see the Prologue, 1.4–9), which he uses three times as much as the other Gospel-writers. What all these examples demonstrate is one of the primary aims of the Gospels: to persuade that Jesus is God, and so to persuade us that God is with us, and so to assure us that we need not fear.

This was just the kind of consolidation Tim had been hoping for, but by now he was ready to do a bit more work with the text. Abi also was fascinated by this new insight into the author's vocabulary and use of symbols. Their next activity was to look for some of the other 30 or so occurrences of the word group of 'glory' in John's Gospel and to see if they bore out what had just been claimed.

Matthew and Luke

What we see is that within the overriding agenda there are local agendas. In the Gospels of Matthew and Luke we can see these agendas played out in the early chapters describing the birth of Jesus and the beginning of his ministry. Matthew 1.1–17 is rarely read in public, but it tells us a great deal about the Gospel that follows, and the understanding of just who Jesus is, in the same way that an overture contains hints of the themes to follow in a piece of music. Matthew's genealogy traces Jesus through Joseph's line (so not a true genealogy) back to Abraham, the father of the Jews. The history is set out in a very stylized way using number symbolism.

TO DO

Read Matthew 1.1–17. Why do you think he places such emphasis on the numbers?

The answer is probably to do with the apocalyptic writers of whom we have heard. One of the features of their writing, which was very popular at the time of Jesus and particularly current among the people to whom Matthew is writing, is an attempt to imbue their words with mystery through using codes. Number codes were very common. So 7, the number of days in the week, and its multiples had special significance. Within this scheme, because it completes creation, seven is the number of God. Eight is generally the number of Jesus, the first in a new creation. The numerical value of David's name in Hebrew is also 14.

In the equivalent passage in Luke (Luke 3.21–38), the genealogy moves in the opposite direction. There are few names in common, no significant numbers and the final ancestor of Jesus is not Abraham, father of the Jews, but Adam, father of humankind and son of God, as he is described. Comparisons show the different interests of the authors. Luke's Gospel has a comprehensive, expansive, inclusive feel. Salvation is for all humankind. Matthew's Gospel is first and foremost for Jews. And so in Matthew's Gospel, Jesus' birth mirrors that of Moses. Both escape genocidal tyrants. Both are hidden in Egypt. One of Matthew's first reports of Jesus' teaching is one of the five collections that give the Gospel such a Jewish literary feel, in chapters 5–7, the so-called Sermon on the Mount. This echoes the account of how Moses received the Law on Mount Sinai. The characteristic feature of the sermon is Jesus' redefinition of the Jewish Law: 'you have heard it said … but I say to you …' (Matthew 5.21–48). The equivalent passage in Luke states specifically that Jesus was not on a mountain but on level ground (6.17). Luke wants to make a link between Jesus and Samuel rather than with Moses. Mary's famous song (Magnificat) in Luke 1.46–55, bears a strong resemblance to the song of Hannah, Samuel's mother in 1 Samuel 2.1–10. Both Matthew and Luke are keen to make the link between Jesus and David. Bethlehem is David's city, and one of the few things that Matthew's and Luke's birth accounts have in common is that Jesus was born there. For Matthew, it is important to find Old Testament proof texts that demonstrate that what is being described is what was once prophesied in the Old Testament. This is a feature of his Gospel, with most texts appearing either at his birth or his passion.

TO DO

Read Matthew 1.18 to the end of chapter 2. How many of these 'proof texts' can you find. How convincing are they for you?

A quick glance through Matthew 1 and 2 will show several places where the formula 'this happened in order to fulfil what was said by the prophet' occurs. These are problematic to scholarship for a number of reasons. One is that by today's standards they fail to convince. Another is that in at least one case we can't find the original reference. Most famously, Matthew probably misunderstands the thrust of the best known of these so-called logion proofs, that is, in 1.22f. The Hebrew of Isaiah 7.14 simply reads, 'young woman of marriageable age', or damsel, as we might say in old English. However, there is no distinction in Greek between this kind of person, on the one hand, and a virgin in the modern or technical sense on the other. Matthew, working from a Greek translation, appears to make a rather clumsy comparison. Alice was shocked by this discovery. She asked whether this meant that the idea of a virgin birth was being challenged. Ken said that the tradition about a virgin birth did not rely on Matthew's translation skills. It was also to be found in Luke's Gospel and was probably widespread in early Christian tradition. What he thought it wiser not to say was that virgin birth could itself be a literary or cultural convention: a way of ascribing divinity rather than a report of historical fact.

But the good news of God's presence and interest is not confined, in the New Testament, to descriptions of the incarnation and its significance and to christological argument. The ongoing presence and interest of God is described in terms of the Holy Spirit.

The Holy Spirit

The Spirit of God is an important concept in Old Testament thought, and that is the primary source for its use and development in the New Testament as well. The Spirit of God appears around 100 times in the Old Testament as a description of God's presence and power, and that number increases if we recognize that the Hebrew word for Spirit can also be translated 'breath' or 'wind'. It has a special connection with prophecy and in the period between the Testaments the Spirit of God develops a special connection also with the

Wisdom of God. Only three times in the Old Testament is the Spirit called 'holy'. In the New Testament generally we may say that the Holy Spirit develops to be a major theme. Paul alone uses the term more than the whole of the Old Testament. It still represents the power of God, and what we might call the creative energy of God, and it retains its connections with both prophecy and Wisdom. In that sense it becomes more obviously one of God's media.

The Holy Spirit does not feature much in the Gospels of Matthew and Mark (five times in Matthew, four in Mark). However, it occurs 53 times in Luke and Acts, two books that are generally accepted as coming from the same author. Ken said that this was perhaps a good example of what the group had been learning: that different authors phrase their arguments in different ways using different images and vocabulary.

TO DO

Read the following passages in Matthew which use the term Holy Spirit: 1.18; 1.20; 3.11; 12.32; 28.19. Can you draw any conclusions about what Holy Spirit means to Matthew from these references? Now read Luke 10.21; 11.13; 12.12. What is introduced here that is new?

For Luke, the Holy Spirit is the source of the early Church's expansion and determination against the odds. It is the means by which the early Church tests its own perceptions of what is right in terms of, for example, the development of ministry or which areas were right for missionary expansion. Importantly, the Spirit is also the source of power with which the disciples are filled at Pentecost. For an example of this you could read the short passage Acts 6.1–6, in which the word Spirit occurs twice at key points, in a context of the inauguration of a new ministry.

John also makes the connection between the Spirit and the launch of the Church. At John 20.22 Jesus reveals himself to the disciples. He bids them peace and commissions them with the words, 'As the

Father sent me, so I send you'; then he breathed on them and said 'Receive the Holy Spirit'. In Hebrew, as we have seen, the same word translates the English, spirit, wind and breath, allowing for some interesting double allusions throughout the Fourth Gospel. One of John's particular developments is found in three passages in his Gospel: at 14.16–26; 15.26f. and 16.7–15, Jesus promises that the Spirit will be a paraclete (Greek: *parakletos*). This is an unusual word, which has primary reference to a court of law. Perhaps the closest parallel would be to the original idea of the so-called soldier's friend in a court martial: that is, one who stands alongside and speaks for you in adversity or when challenged. So the English translates variously, 'advocate' (linking to the court of law context) and 'comforter' (linking to the pastoral role). In addition, the paraclete is a guarantor of truth and, through its support for those who speak God's truth, convicts the world that is content to live in darkness and untruth. As with all manifestations of the Spirit, the paraclete will be a teacher, a means of God's revelation and a guarantor of his presence.

Paul and the Spirit

The other major New Testament source for references to the Holy Spirit is the Epistles of Paul. At this point Ken said the group really was going to enter new ground as it moved from the Gospels to the Epistles or Letters, and he felt that a few words of introduction were probably necessary.

The two things that often come as a surprise to new students of the Letters, he said, are these: first, that the Letters of Paul (Pauline Letters) predate the Gospels; and second, that some of the Letters ascribed to Paul in some Bibles are probably not by him at all. The genuine Letters of Paul are thought to have been written between 49 and 64. The first Gospel (usually taken to be Mark) is commonly dated around 64. What these Letters give us is an insight into the more immediate aftermath of the first Easter, and the formation of early Christian communities. The bridge between the exploits of

Jesus and the exploits of the early Church is the book of Acts, the second volume of Luke's work, which describes the expansion of the Christian Church under the successive leadership of Peter and Paul. That book prepares us for descriptions of church life in places far removed from the original setting of Jesus' ministry. In fact, it does more than that. It helps us to enter conversations going on between different cultures: the one seeking ways to convey good news in categories intelligible to those unfamiliar with Jewish ways of thinking; and the other, questioning the tradition from the standpoint of those who have their own religious heritage and vocabulary. Those conversations, the substance of the Letters, show us how Christian theology was first attempted, how evangelism was conducted, what the actual priorities were for early Christian communities and what Christian communication of the gospel involves. They are examples of applied theology.

Letters are an extremely unusual, probably unique, feature of holy writ in any religion. Inclusion of this material in the New Testament alongside accounts of Jesus' ministry is fascinating and revealing of how the new religion was fundamentally understood. Just to get the feel of the Letters, Ken asked the group to read 1 Corinthians 8. This, he said, was obviously the answer to a question. Ken then asked the group to engage with the following activity.

TO DO

Try and write the part of the letter Paul might have received asking him about this issue. See what general theological truths you can discern Paul pointing to, as he replies to what looks like a very mundane, ordinary and practical dilemma.

Paul is the prime mover in all this, and often thought of as the Church's first theologian. Of the Letters ascribed to him in older Bibles, there is virtually universal agreement that Hebrews is not Pauline. Romans, Corinthians and Galatians are generally regarded as the genuine Letters that tell us most about Paul and his theology.

The First Letter to the Thessalonians is thought to be genuine, but belonging to a relatively undeveloped period of Paul's thinking. Recently, though, there has been renewed interest in its form. The Second Letter to the Thessalonians may be genuine, though that is doubted by some. Another group of Letters, Philippians, Colossians and Philemon, are sometimes called 'the captivity Epistles', on the grounds that they appear to have been written from prison. Ephesians is sometimes included in this group, though the authorship is not certain. Many scholars believe that this was written after Paul's death, by someone writing in his tradition and using some of his idioms, but referring to situations that only became acute after his lifetime. There is even more doubt about the so-called Pastoral Epistles to Timothy and Titus. These, along with Ephesians, are sometimes referred to as deutero-Pauline (that is, the second generation of Pauline theology).

In all Paul's Letters we see evidence of his own immersion in the faith and traditions of Judaism, a deeply informed interest in contemporary theological debate in religious circles generally, and an informed curiosity about the cultures to which his Letters are sent. Religious vocabulary is used from each of these situations and it is not always clear how Paul would want us to understand the terms he is using. However, it is clear that from the Old Testament background, Paul has an understanding of the Spirit such that it is the Spirit of God: that it is singular and unique and in relationship with God. There are not lots of Holy Spirits within a spirit-filled universe of some sort, as some religions might hold. There is just one Spirit, and that Spirit represents God. In fact, Paul uses this singularity to argue for unity within the Church (1 Corinthians 12.4–13). Also from the Old Testament he maintains the link between the Spirit and Wisdom (1 Corinthians 2.10–16), and the essential link between Spirit and prophecy (1 Corinthians 14.1).

The power of the Spirit is commended by Paul, in terms similar to Luke's, as empowering those to whom its gifts have been given. This is particularly true of evangelism and preaching (1 Thessalonians 1.4–6; Romans 15.19; Galatians 3.2). The Spirit can be described, almost interchangeably with the Spirit of God, in this role, as the

Spirit of Christ (Romans 8.9; cf. 8.14). It is this Spirit that brings new life and energy. The Christian life is, hence, life in the Spirit. It is a God-filled life (Romans 8.1–4). It is known by the fruits of the Spirit: of love, joy, peace, patience, kindness, goodness, fidelity, gentleness and self-control (Galatians 5.22f.). This life, dominated by the Spirit, is contrasted on the one hand with living under the law, and on the other with living according to the flesh. The Spirit is in fact the engine of all religious life, for Paul providing the gifts that are required for worship and the building up of the Church.

Doing theology

This may remind us of the kind of thing that John was trying to capture with his vocabulary about eternal life. For him, that was a quality of life lived in the present giving a foretaste of what life in union with God is really like. Paul's Spirit vocabulary has a similar function. It describes life in Christ in the present but offers a foretaste of what God is really like, with perhaps (as some commentators would argue) a more eschatological, future-oriented aspect than John offers. Effectively this is a way of talking about God that precludes the need for extended historical reference to Jesus and his ministry – a reference that is almost totally absent in Paul. The main exception is in 1 Corinthians 11.23ff. where Paul reports a tradition of the Lord concerning the Lord's Supper or Eucharist, but this is rare. For Paul, Spirit vocabulary is about energy, power, prophecy and the dynamism at the heart of the Christian enterprise. It is about that which works for good and is opposed to all that deadens. Here the presence of God is seen not just as a comfort and consolation, but as an inspiration and an aspiration.

TO DO

If you were trying to find a way of expressing the dynamic sense of God's presence and the value it adds to life altogether nowadays, in the way that John and Paul are trying to do in their own time, would you prefer to talk about 'eternal life' or 'the Holy Spirit', or could you think of some other more modern way of describing what you think they want to convey. In shaping and sharing your ideas, you are actually 'doing' theology.

Of the other New Testament texts, the most significant for mention of the Spirit are 1 Peter and Revelation. A major theme in 1 Peter is consolation in the face of unmerited suffering, but that consolation comes primarily from believing that Christ has followed a similar path before the Christians addressed in the Letter and understands their situation completely. The identification between Christ and the believer in 1 Peter comes through baptism, and within that understanding the role of the Spirit is to consecrate and make holy. Only an evidently holy life can be an antidote to evil.

It was 'On the Lord's day [that] the Spirit came upon me' (Revelation 1.10), according to the book of Revelation. In other words, the whole book is placed firmly in the tradition and culture of Old Testament prophecy, from which it borrows freely. The conventions of this kind of writing allow the author to include fantastic visions and auditions as he too addresses problems of suffering and institutionalized evil, with which early Christians are struggling. Most commentators would see the book as belonging to the Old Testament genre of apocalyptic, one feature of which is to try to persuade people whose faith has been strained to the utmost and who wonder if God will ever intervene in their miserable lives that in fact he is still interested and involved.

Conclusion

Ken apologized for packing a few new things in at the end of the session. What we have been talking about today, he said, is an extension of the academic studies we have already seen introduced as Christology and, to some extent, eschatology, with a new -ology to describe the thinking about the Holy Spirit – pneumatology. We have had a chance to look in more detail at some critical issues and themes, and seen more of how the academic business of theology is carried on. We have looked at some of the links between Old and New Testaments and seen how different writers approach their task with different symbols, vocabulary and allusions to make their points. This progression in thinking has led to our having a brief introduction to the Letters of Paul, and brief mention of some other New Testament works. I hope it has not seemed too confusing, he said. Such a wide range of ideas and concerns would not normally be treated together. These have been, so as not to lose sight of a theme that in a sense connects them: namely that part of the good news of Christianity is that God is with us, that God is with us in a way that Old Testament people would recognize, but that God's presence now has a new vitality which will sustain a church. This is the message that maintains the oldest piece of religious good news there is: I am with you. Do not be afraid.

Conversations with the scholars

A good Bible dictionary is probably quite useful here. The companion volume to the one already mentioned is Hawthorne, Martin and Reid (1993), *Dictionary of Paul and his Letters*. A useful and gentle introduction to the Letters of Paul is Horrell (2006), *An Introduction to the Study of Paul* (2nd edn). Commentaries on, and introductions to, the Gospel of John can appear very daunting. One accessible commentary that has stood the test of time is Marsh (1968), *Saint John: The Pelican Gospel Commentaries*. A short introduction by a leading John scholar is Brown (1988), *The Gospel and Epistles of John:*

A Concise Commentary. For a more recent but readable approach, try Carter (2006), *John: Storyteller, Interpreter, Evangelist.*

Further reading

Brown, R. E., 1988, *The Gospel and Epistles of John: A Concise Commentary*, Collegeville, MN: The Liturgical Press.

Carter, W., 2006, *John: Storyteller, Interpreter, Evangelist*, Peabody, MA: Hendrickson.

Hawthorne, G. F., Martin, R. P. and Reid, D. G., 1993, *Dictionary of Paul and his Letters*, Leicester: InterVarsity Press.

Horrell, D. G., 2006, *An Introduction to the Study of Paul*, 2nd edn, London: T. and T. Clark.

Marsh, J., 1968, *Saint John: The Pelican Gospel Commentaries*, London: Penguin Books.

5

The Big Society

Good news, bad news and community

One of Ken's favourite themes proposed that a way of finding out what is good news is to think about what bad news sounds like and then to imagine its opposite. It was largely on this basis that Tim had put something on his list about people being able to live together in harmony. He had decided that it is good news that creative human community is possible, precisely because there is ample evidence to the contrary. On the one hand, there are questions concerning whether individualism and privatization have rendered community impossible to create. Some people blame technological innovation for the lack of commitment to human contact. Old established communities are seen on the TV news having descended into chaos and riots. Tim felt he was beginning to sound like a grumpy old man, but Abi agreed. In her experience, even when communities are formed they are constantly undermined by disagreements, conflict and petty concerns that have a disillusioning effect on those for whom the concept of community is an ideal in its own right. That had been true with the reading group she had been part of, as well as the Community Watch Committee she had tried to set up. She had even seen evidence of it in her church, though she steered well clear of what she had heard described as 'church politics'.

> **TO DO**
>
> Join this conversation with Abi, Tim and the rest. Does evidence of a creative human community come to you as good news? Are you doubtful about it, and what has influenced your views?

Following this initial discussion, Ken summed up: there are conflicting philosophies about how communities can work. For example, should they form around a common purpose? Should there be an element of advantage and reward involved? Are they the more successful the more exclusive they are? And, he said, the Bible has a number of contributions to make here. He started with the Old Testament. Here we have the story of a human community called Israel. It is bound together, latterly at least, by ethnic ties, but more importantly from the perspective of the Bible, by its being part of a covenant relationship with God that defines its identity and purpose. This covenant theology is still important in the New Testament. In fact the Greek word that we translate 'testament' actually means 'covenant'. The New Testament is nothing less than a New Covenant, and he asked the group to read Matthew 26.28; 2 Corinthians 3.6; 3.14 and Hebrews 8.7–13.

Bible communities keep in touch

As a result of disillusion about the possibility of creative and just human community, first the Old Testament prophets and later the intertestamental writers, dream of an ideal society that has particular characteristics. They referred to this as the Kingdom of God, and that is the centrepiece of Jesus' teaching. The question then arises: where does the Church fit into all this? For New Testament writers, the Church itself is clearly meant to be a new attempt at creative human community, but there is debate among scholars about what are its antecedents, how it describes itself, how it orders itself, what sustains its life and how successful it is. After all, there is ample evidence in the book of Acts, or in 1 Corinthians and elsewhere, that the early Church's story was stuttering and characterized often by failure. But that does not prevent writers from holding a vision of the Church as an ideal society.

The Gospels tell us the story of God's purposes by telling us the story of Jesus. The rest of the New Testament attempts to do so, mostly, by telling us the story of the Church. At times these two stories are interwoven with each other, but certainly the New Testament Letters give us an insight into the nature and purpose of faith communities, which is why those communities have preserved them and value them. Ken said there is a real link here with the idea of good news because, just like the Gospels, the Letters are meant to be news. Indeed they can be big news, providing as they do evidence of God's continuing work and power.

Just to recap, Ken said that scholars usually divide the material of the New Testament into six categories:

- the Gospels and Acts;
- the Letters of Paul that are universally accepted as genuine;
- other letters ascribed to Paul, in his tradition, but from a later date – sometimes called deutero-Pauline. There is disagreement among scholars about which books belong in this group;
- Catholic Letters: that is, letters written to a general rather than a specific audience. That is the significance of the word 'catholic', whose basic meaning is 'universal';
- Johannine Letters – a subgroup of the Catholic Letters: that is, the three letters that are in the tradition of John;
- the book of Revelation, which is in a category of its own, sometimes described as New Testament apocalyptic, though not everyone agrees that it is an apocalypse in the traditional sense.

> ## TO DO
>
> To get the feel of these different divisions, read a chapter of a book from each of them. You might try: 1 Corinthians 2; Titus 1; James 1; 1 John 3; Revelation 19. What do you think about the variety of what you have read? Which are you more attracted to? Which would you like to know more about?

Ken said that in order to see two different ways of describing the Church in the New Testament (scholars call this study *ecclesiology*), the group would look at two New Testament books in particular: 1 Corinthians and 1 Peter. Each gives tantalizing clues about the early Church, its ministry, order, worship, identity, expectations and relation to context, and each is written by an author with a creative passion about the role and possibility of the Church. But more than that, looking at these books will allow us to see a number of different approaches to the study of the non-Gospel material in the New Testament. Ken asked if there were any questions from the group based on what they had read and heard and shared already that the group needed to deal with before looking at the texts.

Questions about letters

Abi asked if other religions had letters as part of their holy writings, because, she said, it seemed very strange to her. As she had been reading, she had been struck by just how personal, like her own letters, some parts of them had been. Tim asked why the churches addressed had kept them, and could it be that some had been lost. Alice had read all the suggested passages carefully and had noticed that there were many different pictures used to describe the Church. Why is that, she asked, and how many are there? Ken said he would deal, as best he could, with those questions first.

- Indeed, we might reflect that letters are a strange medium for holy writings. Generally, letters of any kind are not meant for posterity. In fact, they are valuable in that they are so immediately related to their time and place. They are hardly suitable media for theological treatises, sermons, sustained narrative or philosophical reflection. But what letters can do is present us with a dynamic picture of their circumstances. They are often personal to the point of being passionate. They are a real means of connection between congregations. They are suitable for answering queries raised or maintaining dialogue about an issue. They can bear the weight of conveying argument and rhetoric.

- The fact that they have been kept and revered points us to something else that is important. The early Church needed instruments of unity. It needed some kind of oversight, particularly as the apostles themselves began to die. We have to imagine relatively small scattered congregations, all over the Mediterranean and Middle East, founded in different ways, with different theological priorities and different styles. Simply reading the New Testament nowadays can blind us to the fact that the early Church was a very loose coalition. What was to hold it together? The answer was shared traditions and strong external leadership – a leadership that was itself aware of the need to build some common theological bases, establish some common practices and encourage recognizable structures among the several congregations and cultures. The person of Paul and the writings of Paul, for example, show evidence of providing just that.

- That is not to say that Paul wanted to impose just one idea or one central bureaucracy. He is quite happy to work with variety up to a point. And indeed, one example of that is the number of pictures he draws to describe the Church. It is the Body of Christ. Believers are ambassadors, the Israel of God, a letter, soldiers of Christ. In the New Testament as a whole, one modern scholar has found 96 different pictures of the Church. In those circumstances, questions about what they have in common are bound to arise, and some kind of arbitration within doctrinal disputes and questions is likely to be needed. We see all that within the letters, and that is part of what has made them a valuable resource for the church ever since.

TO DO

If you were to pick up a letter nowadays and told to study it, what questions would you want to ask in order to make sense of that letter and fully describe it to someone else? Make a list and then see how it compares with what scholars do, as outlined below.

Writing to Corinth

The First Letter to the Corinthians is perhaps the Letter of Paul that gives us the best insight into the practical everyday life of a Mediterranean congregation that is far removed geographically and culturally from the lands of Jesus' ministry. It is also a good example of how the traditional historical-critical approach to the Letters has produced good results.

That approach might seem to be the natural one to adopt, since it mirrors the way in which we would make sense of a letter we might receive nowadays. We would look at the postmark to see where it has come from and when. Then we would perhaps check the address to see for whom it was intended. On opening it, our first interest would be who sent it, and we would want to read the letter to find out why they had sent it. It might be a letter we were expecting, in answer to one we had sent. If a third party were to pick that up, she or he would have to second guess, from the answer, what the question might have been. This series of questions is the one that has characterized study of the Letters.

In the case of the New Testament Letters there are some further questions to ask. Is the letter as we have it a unity, or might it be a letter cobbled together with some other kind of writing – a sermon or a treatise or an order of service? Has the correspondence been edited, so that what appears to be one letter is in fact a collection from different times and circumstances, and are all the contributions from the same author? At least in the case of 1 Corinthians those questions have been answered in ways that have gained general acceptance. It is thought to be just one letter. The Second Letter to the Corinthians, on the other hand, may be a collection of two or three letters gathered together. The key thing is that the Letters are treated in just the same way as historians would deal with other ancient letters, looking for both internal and external evidence to reach conclusions on the kind of questions raised above.

One issue of interpretation concerns the weight we attach to the account of Paul's travels and ministry in the Acts of the Apostles. There was a time when this book was seen as a straightforward account, much like a modern history, of what really happened. But as Acts was accepted as part two of Luke's Gospel, so scholars became more aware of its agendas and rhetorical intent. That is not to say that it is historically worthless, however, and in the case of 1 Corinthians there is a strong correlation between the account in Acts and what we see in the Letter. Paul founded the Corinthian church (Acts 18.1–11), and a comparison of Acts 18.27—19.1 with 1 Corinthians 3.5–10 connects Apollos in both cases. However, the best evidence for Paul's authorship is the fact that it was accepted without question by a later Bishop of Rome, Clement, writing to the church in Corinth some 40 years later, who makes reference to 'the epistle of the blessed Paul' and to which his own letter is a kind of sequel (*1 Clement* 47.1–3).

It is interesting to see how scholars date letters. Acts 18.2 says that Paul met Priscilla and Aquila in Corinth after Emperor Claudius had expelled the Jews from Rome. This expulsion is usually dated AD 49, making the date of Paul's first visit to Corinth around 50. The reference to Gallio (Acts 18.12ff.) gives us a date of 51/52, confirming the historicity of the Acts account and providing a date for Paul's stay in Corinth of 50–52. What scholars have then done is to piece together the events that took place in Paul's life, and the life of the church, attested in Acts, between that first visit and the writing of the letter to arrive at a date of around 55 for the letter.

The Corinthian church

Tim interrupted to ask if this was the method that was used to begin study of all the New Testament Letters and whether it was equally successful with all of them. Ken said that because we had an alternative source for the travels of Paul in Acts, the method was most successful with Paul's writings and was able to give us a reasonably reliable timeline of his writings, though often these were quite conjectural. One recent such attempt would put Galatians first of the Letters (*c.* 45), 1 and 2 Thessalonians *c.* 50, 1 and 2 Corinthians 54/55, Romans sometime between then and 59, and the Captivity Letters and disputed Letters, if they are by Paul, between 60 and 64.

Ken continued: partly on account of this, it is generally accepted that Paul wrote 1 Corinthians from Ephesus, in response to queries brought to him (perhaps by those mentioned in 1 Corinthians 16.17, perhaps by Apollos (16.12)), as described at 7.1. These queries he answers directly, but their very nature raises deeper theological questions for him about unity in the Church and about the extent to which the Corinthians have actually grasped the essence of this new religion. Part of the misunderstandings and partial understandings can be understood better if we consider what it was like to live in Corinth in those days. And again a historical approach can help us, because there are external sources sufficient for us to have a full picture of that.

We have to imagine 'old Corinth', by then just a deserted ruin, and 'new Corinth', bustling and cosmopolitan as a result of the opening of the Corinth canal cutting across the narrowest isthmus of the Peloponnese peninsula. It was a place for new money, and a place where retired soldiers were resettled. It had a reputation for moral decadence. 'To play the Corinthian' was a well-known description of moral laxity. It was a place where the famous came, and which needed a large number of 'downstairs' people to service it all. To a culture which is used to heroes, personalities and celebrities, the self-effacing approach of Paul must have been puzzling. To a place built on all the worldly pillars of success and optimism, the theology of Christ, a God who was crucified, must have indeed been folly and a stumbling block (1 Corinthians 1.22f). But we are fortunate in that the church at Corinth got almost everything about being a Christian church wrong, so that we can see from Paul's responses what he thinks a church in the world might look like at best.

Ken asked the group to judge what similarities and differences there might be between the society of Corinth he had described and a modern place of which members had experience. Someone called Justin, who had recently returned from employment in Dubai kept the group entertained with some of his memories, but others found connections with the places where they lived now.

TO DO

Join in the discussion. What similarities and differences do you see between the society of Corinth and a modern place that you know well?

Among the topics addressed by Paul we find apologetic sections, defending Christianity against contemporary philosophy (1 Corinthians 1.18—2.16), alongside a corrective about the nature of baptism (1.10–17). Chapters 3 and 4 give us a number of pictures of the Church. These include the Church as God's garden, God's building, God's temple, stewards of the secrets of God, fools for Christ's sake, Paul's offspring, the Kingdom of God, and even, intriguingly, as the last act in the show (4.9). This brief list from just two chapters shows the vitality of creative thinking about what exactly the Church is and how it can be described, he said. From chapter 5 onwards Paul turns to the answers to specific problems.

These succeeding chapters present a sorry tale to which Paul responds robustly, and in the process does creative theology. Chapter 10, for example, begins with some startling universal and inclusive statements as a prelude to what he has to say about old religious ideas and certainties (described as idolatry), also saying something about seemingly banal matters such as hair regulations in the new religion and, as a climax, teaching on the conduct of a Eucharist or Communion service. It is worth just giving what might seem banal or irrelevant to us a little context. Almost all world religions are accompanied by regulations about food, hairstyle and the right relations between the sexes. That is still the case today. In the seventh century, one of the great moments in the history of the Church in Britain, the Synod of Whitby, which determined the shape of church life for centuries, could have been described as a dispute about haircuts. It was actually a radical step to deal with these issues as Paul does and to point to new priorities.

Certainly one of the chief of these is the sense of community that is evidenced and celebrated in the Eucharist. In chapters 10 and 11 Paul uses one of the new theological terms with which he is associated – *koinonia* – which can be translated 'communion', 'sharing' or 'fellowship'. This is part of his wider understanding of the theology of the Body of Christ, in which all belong together in an organic way. What clearly offends him is yet another misunderstanding in Corinth. It seems that the Communion is celebrated there in connection with some other social function in which food is eaten. The well-off eat well and the poor go without, and then they have a Eucharist. This is a complete contradiction in terms for Paul and he is quick to say so (11.17–22). The positive side for us is that Paul then feels constrained to set out how it *should* be done, and in the process gives us the earliest and clearest description of what has become the Church's Communion service.

TO DO

How happy would Paul be with the services in your own church? What would Paul want to write to your church?

So what we see here, Ken said in conclusion, is that historical method has given us a specific actual geographical, temporal and cultural context with which to interpret what is undoubtedly a genuine work of Paul. We see how he does theology, allowing context to be the engine of creative new words and actions representing something that can be sharply defined when it is abused, even though there is room for a variety of interpretations. It is this historical method that has been the basis for making sense of the Letters for most of the twentieth century and into the present century and that is responsible for much of what we think we know about them. This is the method that will be encountered in any 'critical introduction' textbook.

1 Peter

When historical method is applied to 1 Peter it is unfortunately less successful. In many respects this book belongs with the Pauline Letters on account of its sharp and distinctive theology, but many would place it with the deutero-Pauline material. After 2,000 years there is still considerable debate about virtually every aspect of this book. There is no agreement about who wrote it, when it was written, where it was written, or whether it was all written at once by the same person. There are a variety of views about whether it is a letter or not, and about both the purpose and the occasion of the writing. Yet there is agreement that 1 Peter contains valuable material about the nature of the early Church community.

It may be helpful to give the flavour of some of the arguments. On the face of it, two main themes of 1 Peter are baptism and suffering (or perhaps more accurately, worship and suffering). Some have concluded that this is either a baptismal liturgy or baptismal homily, making passing references to suffering. Others have said this is a document offering succour to those undergoing persecution and reminding them in passing of baptismal vows.

Ken invited his group to look at some of the key passages. If you want to stress baptism, he said, then you point to the possible reference to the Trinity in 1.1–2, the references to becoming holy in 1.13–15, the possible reference in 1.22f. to a baptism just having taken place, and the references to Christian infancy at the beginning of chapter 2. The extended reference to the place of lay people in the Church in chapter 2 would fit with something delivered to those who have just become members of it through baptism, as would the household code (a technical term) in 3.1–9. There is a specific reference to baptism in 3.21.

TO DO

Join in the task and examine passages that stress suffering: 1.6f.; 2.18–23; 3.13–18; 4.1f.; 4.12–16; 5.8–10. You might also want to judge whether this is two documents or one. Some scholars think the break comes after 4.11. Can you see why they should think that?

You might think that the question of authorship is fairly straight-forward. Why should we think anything other than that Peter wrote it? Well, Peter was a simple fisherman and the Greek in 1 Peter is among the most sophisticated in the New Testament. Also, if Peter wrote it, clearly it must have been before his death in 64, and some scholars believe that the theology of 1 Peter fits better with a later date and that the kind of persecution and suffering described in the book appears to be closer to events documented elsewhere in 112 than in Nero's persecutions of the early 60s. It is also claimed that the internal literary evidence (where the Letter seems to draw on a fund of common catechetical material used for teaching new converts) points to a later date. It is possible from a passing comment in the book (5.12) that it was ghostwritten by Silvanus, which might overcome some objections. Others think this to be a pseudonymous document from the early second century.

What sociology offers

Given this confusion, scholars have turned to other critical approaches to open up the book, and one that has provided interesting results is the so-called socio-scientific approach.

Social scientific criticism is not completely new and different in principle, but is rather a complement to other critical approaches. It attempts to bring the insights of the social sciences to bear on texts, and to see how texts both reflect and respond to the social and cultural milieus that produced them. This relies on a certain kind of historical enquiry about what life was like. It is also interested in the formation and transmission of texts in so far as that is related to particular social situations. Did the lower classes chatter the gospel or did the upper classes write about it. The social make-up of Jesus' followers, and the way they might have understood and interpreted references to contemporary issues, is one aspect of this study. The social make-up of the early Church is another. Was it mostly composed of the well to do, or was it mostly a lower-class thing? Was it predominantly urban or rural, and so on? As with redaction critics, though, social scientific critics tend to concentrate on the final form of the text. Their work is meant to be an aid to both exegesis (that is, drawing out the meaning of a text) and hermeneutic (that is, explaining and interpreting the text as an exercise in communication).

One thing that is clear from 1 Peter is that from a sociological point of view the addressees are relatively powerless. Their Christian discipleship is to be demonstrated not in giving alms or exercising influence, but rather in suffering silently and showing dignity in the face of abuse (2.11–15; 3.8–18; 4.7–10; 4.12–16). The addressees are urged to live *as* if they were freemen (2.16) and to submit to their masters (2.18), but there is no word as to how masters should behave. One study has explored the terms used throughout the letter to describe those addressed, and found that *paroikia* (aliens) and *parapidemoi* (exiles) in particular were almost technical terms for a particular class of person in Asia Minor throughout the period in question. Often this been interpreted in a spiritual way. Christians are citizens of heaven, therefore they are exiles on earth. A social scientific approach takes the actual social description seriously and so sees the people as rather like guest-workers in some countries today. That is, they were people with no rights of citizenship, forced to do the worst jobs, among the most likely to be abused, exploited, trafficked or ill-treated. Essentially they were people without a home. The social strategy of the book, it is claimed, is to assure these homeless people that they have a home. The Church is their spiritual house of which they are all a part. There is an *oikos* for the *paroikos*.

This approach raises new questions as we seek to understand and apply the book's message. What we would then be interested in is not 'Peter's view of church based on his experience', but rather, 'what kind of church, and what understanding of church is appropriate in such social circumstances'.

What we actually find is a remarkable and distinctive picture of church, based not on hierarchy or authority but rather a picture that takes some of the most distinctive epithets of the community of faith from the Old Testament and reapplies them to the whole community or congregation of Christians. They are a spiritual temple, a holy priesthood, a chosen race, a royal priesthood, a dedicated nation and God's own people (1 Peter 2.4–10). They are living stones. This is one of the most radical descriptions of church to be found anywhere in the New Testament. It demonstrates continuity between Old and New Testaments by radically redefining the whole nature of what the originals signified. To put it bluntly and perhaps oversimply: people are the essence of the Church, not buildings.

The people of God

God's chosen are not defined by ethnic origin but by their transparent faith as it translates into faithful obedience. We no longer have the holy man, the holy season and the holy ritual. Instead we have what has been described as 'the priesthood of all believers'. This is an even more radical concept than that English translation might imply. This is not 'the priesthood of each believer'. It is priesthood represented and concentrated in the whole community. From now on, those who lead a congregation do so not because they are uniquely conferred with divine authority, but rather because they represent a community conferred with divine authority. People are doing it for themselves. And this is a concept of church that is well suited to a congregation that knows nothing of power, that needs to be reassured that their suffering has been noticed and that they count in God's eyes, and that is do-able by the servant classes and the marginalized. Social scientific approaches have given us a way into the text that makes it usable and applicable to many contexts in the world today. Ken finished with a triumphant smile.

Conclusion

Abi broke the dramatic silence by asking: what has this got to do with whether a perfect human community is possible? I see it as connecting with what Jesus said about the Kingdom of heaven, said Alice. Perhaps that's why there is so little mention of the Kingdom in the Letters. Perhaps the Church is meant to be the Kingdom. That thought too hung in the air for a while. Tim said, well I want to believe it is possible and, without sounding too pious about it, it's one of the reasons I go to church at all. Ken said, the problem with inspiring ideals and idealists is that they seem to be overtaken always either by human evil and subversion or by the human instinct to make something exciting, challenging and edgy more manageable by institutionalizing it, and there's evidence of that in the New Testament too. But let's stick to the good news. Creative human community is possible.

Conversations with the scholars

In addition to books already mentioned, if you are interested in the social approach to texts you might read Elliott (1993), *What is Social Scientific Criticism?* Also of interest would be Stambaugh and Balch (1986), *The Social World of the First Christians* and Meeks (1983), *The First Urban Christians*. Specifically on 1 Peter, the critical history is well covered by Achtemeier (1996), *1 Peter* (Hermeneia Commentaries). The application of social scientific method to 1 Peter is in the classic study, Elliott (1990), *A Home for the Homeless* (2nd edn), and for this approach in the context of Paul's Letters, Theissen (1982), *The Social Setting of Pauline Christianity.*

A classic study on the variety of ecclesiologies in the New Testament is Schweizer (1961), *Church Order in the New Testament,* and an attempt to put Church development in a historical setting, by a well recognized author, is Trocmé (1997), *The Childhood of Christianity.*

General introductions to Paul include Dunn (2003), *The Cambridge Companion to Saint Paul* (like the other volumes in this series, an excellent collection of essays covering the main agenda of scholars presently). Also Wright (1997), *What St Paul Really Said.* On 1 Corinthians specifically, see Dunn (1995), *1 Corinthians.*

Further reading

Achtemeier, P., 1996, *1 Peter* (Hermeneia Commentaries), Minneapolis, MN: Fortress Press.

Dunn, J. D. G., 1995, *1 Corinthians,* Sheffield: Sheffield Academic Press.

Dunn, J. D. G. (ed.), 2003, *The Cambridge Companion to Saint Paul,* Cambridge: Cambridge University Press.

Elliott, J. H., 1990, *A Home for the Homeless,* 2nd edn, Minneapolis, MN: Fortress Press.

Elliott, J. H., 1993, *What is Social Scientific Criticism?,* Minneapolis, MN: Fortress Press.

Meeks, W., 1983, *The First Urban Christians,* New Haven, CT: Yale University Press.

Schweizer, E., 1961, *Church Order in the New Testament,* London: SCM Press.

Stambaugh, J. and Balch, D., 1986, *The Social World of the First Christians,* London: SPCK.

Theissen, G., 1982, *The Social Setting of Pauline Christianity,* Edinburgh: T. and T. Clark.

Trocmé, E., 1997, *The Childhood of Christianity,* London: SCM Press.

Wright, N. T., 1997, *What St Paul Really Said,* New York: Eerdmans.

6

You Have 27 New Friends

Introduction

The news was that for this session the group was going to be joined by a guest facilitator who was apparently an expert in the field. They had been expecting one of the sessions to have this different structure and be longer, and looked forward to meeting the new person. He turned out to be a middle-aged man called William, whose introduction to himself was so vague and self-effacing that the group wondered where on earth he could be working, and whether in fact he actually knew more about the New Testament than they did.

Getting connected

He began by saying that he wanted to explore how people felt connected with each other. In what he thought was a light aside, he gave the example of a social network site telling him he had 27 new friends. The use of words like 'friends' or 'family' (as in some commercial operations) or 'community' (as in some mobile phone advertising) suggest the ways in which we most prefer to be grouped. Previous generations took words like 'citizens' or 'members' to describe their way of belonging, but essentially they were seeking the same kind of thing. In the New Testament, there is a great deal about belonging, and particularly about the new relationships that are possible between humankind and God. But it is the Church that is the visible instrument of belonging, and as it developed its life by widening its geographical spread, by translating theological ideas into new cultural contexts, by broadening its ministry base and simply by growing older and maturing, it needed to find ways to give a discernible sense of unity to something that was becoming tremendously diverse. So, he said, this good news is about connectedness, and the peace and security that brings. No one could remember writing 'connectedness' on their initial list, but they could see what he was getting at. Then William introduced the following activity.

TO DO

Looking back to your work on the Letters of Paul, write an introduction to an imaginary job description for Paul, summing up what his job is going to be, from the benefit of the hindsight you have.

Tim thought that the description should say something about unity. He had been struck by the way Paul could deal with different expectations and cultures and still end up with something that was recognizably similar. Reflecting on how Paul achieved this, his main thought was about the new theological thinking he brought to the task. That had also appealed to Abi's imagination. For Alice the jury was still out on the theological creativity of the early Church. She did not want to lose sight of the fact for her that God was behind all this. But she did accept that Paul had laid the foundations of new forms of worship and church organization.

William summed up the job description for Paul like this:

To sketch a new common theology and to demonstrate how that could be applied in very different cultures and situations. And to provide new points of reference as to how certain practical things should be done: for example, how a Eucharist should be celebrated or how disciplinary procedures might work, in response to enquiries; and so to begin to put in place some structures and guidelines. This might be described as the beginnings of institutional life.

Then William asked the simple question, do you think these two things are compatible with each other: the new adventure of creative theology and the foundations of institutional life? He gave them some time to split into smaller groups to think about that from their own experience.

TO DO

Join one of those groups. Think of examples from other walks of life of how pioneering idealists have given way to a dead hand of grey institutionalism. You might think of trades union history in several countries, revolutions in countries seeking to escape despotic rule, the feminist movement of the twentieth century, or other examples. Is this progression inevitable do you think?

After Paul

William continued: over a period of time as the Church grew, and as figures of universal authority such as Paul died, the result was to move to a new phase of church development in which order and structure take centre stage. This is most clearly seen in the books that are classed as deutero-Pauline and, he said, these are the writings we shall be looking at today. Within that group, perhaps the movement can be seen most clearly in the so-called Pastoral Epistles: 1 and 2 Timothy and Titus. Let me say first, he went on, why these letters are thought to be later than Paul. There is a series of tests.

The first test is usually to compare vocabulary and style with those of genuine Letters. In the Pastorals there are 306 words not found elsewhere in Paul and 175 not found elsewhere in the New Testament. Then, the themes and ideas of the books are examined to see whether they best fit an early or later phase of church development. Also, attention is paid to how quickly the whole Church accepted the books as genuine works worthy of inclusion in the

New Testament. Books that contain references to opponents give us a further opportunity to date them because the details of the opponents' beliefs can be checked against the known development of sects from other sources. Finally, scholars try to find whether it is possible to place the writing within the life of Paul as that is known from other biographical fragments and accounts. Although some scholars hold to a Pauline authorship for the Pastoral Epistles, the deutero-Pauline solution is most commonly adopted. From the point of view of how we access the contents, it makes little odds, because they are self-evidently very different from the other letters.

TO DO

To see the differences in style and vocabulary, you might read Romans 12 as one description of how churches should regard themselves, and then read 1 Timothy 2.

Abi did this activity and thought the authors came across not just as from different times but as if they lived on different planets. She was still fuming about the description of the place of women as William continued.

Pastoral Letters

These three books have been known as the Pastoral Epistles since 1726. The name derives from the fact that they appear to be written to individual pastors and deal with everyday issues encountered by church leaders. There is far greater anxiety here than in the earlier works about 'false teaching'. The concept of orthodoxy is becoming very important and the use of phrases such as 'sound doctrine' (Titus 2.1) and 'the true Gospel' (2 Timothy 2.15) are more common. There are short passages that look like creeds in the making (1 Timothy 3.16). Church order and discipline are new priorities. There are templates for 'offices' such as bishop or elder

(Titus 1.6–9). Discipline is not restricted to churches. These books also contain so-called household codes, which set out appropriate behaviour between members of Christian families. Here, the household is the chief model for the Church, and this has led to the charge that these books describe 'bourgeois Christianity'. While earlier scholarship concentrated on authorship as the key to interpretation, more recently, scholars have become more interested in their social setting, in the literary form of testimony and in the idea of pastor as a kind of spiritual director.

There was a general discussion about group members' reactions to books they had rarely encountered before. William was perhaps playing devil's advocate in his barely concealed view that this was a retrograde step in the Church's life. The majority view was that, being realistic, if the Church was to have a continuing life, like any human society, it needed things like a constitution and rules. The important thing was not to lose sight of the exciting initial vision. Most group members thought that tension was well maintained in these Letters.

TO DO

Do you agree?

The community that remembered John

Next, they looked at the three Letters of John. William said that these present us with a different picture of early Church life. Here the theological outlook and language is reminiscent of John's Gospel. Much critical energy has been spent on the question of the relationship between the Epistles and the Gospel, as well as on the relationship of the Epistles to each other. The books 2 and 3 John share common agenda. The subject of 2 John is the treatment of itinerant preachers and the subject of 3 John is praise of someone called Gaius for accepting itinerants. It also censures someone called

Diotrephes and speaks positively of one Demetrius. These sound like routine letters written from one church to another, and the questions of who is favoured and who is not will be more than familiar to anyone who has spent much time in a church nowadays. More than in the Letters of Paul, we are brought face to face here with inter-church conflict. In the Gospel of John the 'enemy' is usually identified as either 'the world' or 'the Jews'. Here the enemy is other Christians. Both Letters are written by someone who simply calls himself 'the Presbyter'. Abi thought that sounded rather sinister: a bit like a title for a gangster leader. Certainly institutional church leaders were not having a good day.

The book of 1 John is longer, has no declared author within the text and is more theologically interesting. It shares some vocabulary with the Gospel of John.

TO DO

To get the feel of the similarities between the Gospel and the Letters, and to see the difference between these writings and those of, say, Paul, read John 1.1–14 and then 1 John 1.1–7.

Examples of similarities in these passages and others include reference to: life (John 1.4; 10.10; 1 John 1.2; 5.11f.), light (John 1.4–9; 1 John 1.5; 2.8–10), eternal life (John 3.15f.; 1 John 5.11, 13, 20). A 'new commandment' is spoken of in 1 John 2.7–8, 'which you have had from the beginning', reminiscent of John 13.34. And there are other examples. Some scholars have deduced a common authorship. Some have thought that the body of work had a common editor. Others, following Raymond Brown, have seen the Epistles as work deriving from a 'community of the beloved disciple', giving evidence of what that community was concerned about and how it expressed itself in the second generation.

Disputes in the community

There are two main points of dispute. The first is about how the community views Jesus: that is, it is about Christology. A constant issue within christological discussion is about the exact proportions of divinity and humanity that are to be found in Jesus. William sensed that some members were beginning to glaze over, and so expanded a little. He said, some people thought that Jesus was essentially a human dressed in God's clothes. Others thought the exact opposite, that he was God pretending to be human. This was an issue that exercised the Church greatly during the first five centuries of its existence and that led to splits or schisms, the creation of highly convoluted creeds and the development of the concept of orthodoxy. If Jesus is seen to be more human than divine, then what force do titles like 'Son of God' really have? Was he anything more than another prophet? How could someone like that accomplish anything on the cross apart from setting a heroic example? If, on the other hand, he was more divine than human, then in what sense could that really be described as an incarnation? The position that saw Jesus as more God than man was the more common and led to what was described as a heresy called Docetism. John's Gospel is sometimes cited as giving rise to that kind of thinking, in the sense that Jesus is rarely seen simply doing human things for their own sake. Even when he eats or drinks, the acts are interpreted in a spiritual way. The position of the opponents in 1 John is set out at 4.1–4. The alternative view, which the author is promoting, is described at 5.1 and 5.5. What the author is trying to do is set out a refutation of any view that diminishes the humanity of Jesus, while rehabilitating a view that his humanity was important in the whole drama of salvation.

TO DO

Read 1 John 2.18–29. Now think of any current dispute in the Church, either locally or nationally. Why do you think 'false teaching' was, and continues to be, an issue to be treated with such vehemence?

This is connected to the second area of dispute, which is about ethics. The author's position is that Christian ethics is related to knowledge of Christ, and this is set out especially in the first two chapters (see 1 John 2.4, 6–11). It is interesting that in comparison with the Synoptic Gospels, there is comparatively little straightforward ethical teaching material in John's Gospel and this leaves a gap for the continuing community perhaps. In John's Gospel, ethics is not so much a practical as an intellectual concern. In the Synoptic Gospels there is an emphasis on doing (e.g. Matthew 12.50), whereas at John 8.31 what is required is to 'stand by' teaching (literally, 'if you remain in my word'). There is some mention in 1 John of keeping commands (2.3; 3.22f.; 5.3), but these are related to general statements about love and mirroring the love of God or Christ. The biggest sin is that of not believing. The irony remains, that in an Epistle that places a great emphasis on loving one's brother, the definition of brother should be limited to those who agree with the author's doctrinal position.

In fact, said William, there is a general impression of an insular community from these Letters. 'Love your neighbour' has become 'Love your brother', and there is little that suggests a worldly context for Christian action. Disputes within the Church give an interesting view to historians and dogmatic theologians of how thinking was developing during this second-generation period, but concerns about disputes between the mainstream and the fringes predominate.

A letter of straw?

The Letter of James was the next writing to examine. William said that this had had a controversial history. Martin Luther famously condemned it as an 'Epistle of Straw', and more recently it has been described as the junk mail of the New Testament. One reason for this antipathy is the emphasis that the Letter places on good works rather than a profession of faith. This could be seen to be at odds with Paul's insistence that we are saved by faith, though there have been many attempts to show that the two writers' views are compatible. However, there are other concerns. There is a lack of reference to the saving death and resurrection of Jesus. Actually, Jesus is only mentioned, specifically, twice, and one of those mentions at 2.1 seems quite unconnected with what follows. He is simply not part of the argument. The haphazard style is also a barrier to some, as is suspicion born of the fact that this Epistle had quite a struggle to be accepted as part of the New Testament at all.

Supporters of James say that we must understand the genre of the work to appreciate it. It is a teaching document, they say, and belongs to a technical class of writings called *paraenesis*. This Greek word means 'advice' and is used by New Testament scholars to describe the kind of moral exhortation that belongs to practical living. This would account for its rather disjointed style, and the fact that the Letter does not appear to be addressed to a particular situation. In this kind of writing the author's identity is relatively unimportant – he is principally a collector and collator of sayings and aphorisms. There are said to be many parallels between James and the teaching of Jesus. The fact that they are not described as Jesus' teaching may be an indication of how fully that teaching had become an integrated part of discipleship that needed no further justification. In particular, there are said to be echoes of the Beatitudes, as they appear in Matthew, and in the same order. So, for example, Matthew 5.3 is similar to James 2.5; Matthew 5.7 to James 2.12f.; Matthew 5.9 to James 3.18; and Matthew 5.12 to James 5.10f.

> ## TO DO
>
> Read the Beatitudes in the Matthew version and then look at the supposed parallels in James. As a Bible scholar, what conclusions would you draw from this evidence? Judging by the topics covered and the words used through this Letter, what picture emerges in your mind of the situation that might have demanded it? Who do you think is the audience here?

Some commentators want to claim that James belongs to the genre of Wisdom literature, and it is true that the Letter shares some characteristics with Old Testament Wisdom literature. However, in comparison, it has a rather subversive approach that favours the weak, poor and landless. It also has an eschatological emphasis missing from Wisdom. Some are content to see it as a letter or encyclical. Either there is an attempt to give it a context in Palestine or it is seen as a general series of pieces that address typical situations wherever they may occur. The main themes that are treated include: faith and works (2.14–26); the perils of loose speech and the responsibilities of teaching (3.1–12); friendship with God rather than with the world (4.1–10); social justice (4.11—5.6); and prayer for the suffering and sick (5.13–18).

A complicated letter

The Letter to the Hebrews was next. Once attributed to Paul, it is now virtually universally acknowledged as belonging to a later period. On the face of it, this is probably one of the most inaccessible documents of the New Testament. It is written in a style that is difficult, conveys ideas that are unfamiliar to us and all in a document about whose circumstances of writing hardly anything is known, including details about the author or recipients, or indeed whether it is even a letter at all. On the other hand, it can be justly claimed to be one of the most creative theological documents in the New Testament and most people who have studied it in depth think they have been well repaid. Barnabas Lindars writes: 'Hebrews is rather like the prophet Ezekiel. He appears strange and impersonal and distant at first, but closer acquaintance shows him to be a deeply caring person with a strong pastoral sense' (1991, p. xii).

The Letter does not begin like a letter, even though it ends like one. It shows knowledge of and concern for the recipients and their situation. Teaching is interspersed with encouragement and there are some features (such as alliteration and a dramatic building of phrases) that suggest either that originally some of these texts were spoken or that the author is used to writing speeches or sermons. There is evidence for the circulation of collections of homilies, but these do usually, in other cases, seem to have a particular context and a well-expressed pastoral concern (see, for example, the conclusion of the Letter, 13.20ff.). From the Letter we can deduce some things about the recipients. Older commentators were concerned as to whether they were Jews or Gentiles, but of more interest really is to ask what was their problem. They are a mature community who have witnessed persecution (10.32–34) and who in the past have given generous support, but who have run out of ideas. They once gave well of themselves in charitable work, met frequently and could rely on the commitment of their members. That is no longer true. Now they need inspiration. They are a depressed community (5.11f.) who have given up on the things which are important in churches, like assembly and worship (6.12; 10.34–39). The author of this Letter seeks to rekindle the interest of his readers by framing Christianity in a new theological language and idiom.

TO DO

Try to imagine yourself as a member of a church like this. Once it had a heyday when everything you would expect of a church was happening, but now little is happening and there is general apathy and decline. What is needed to revive it in your view?

There was a general view in the group that leadership was largely to blame. Some people thought that the general culture of society played a part. Others blamed a slackening of zeal by members, perhaps attributable to a lack of inspiration. What do you think of the author of this work's approach, that what they need is to be excited by a new presentation of theology?

The main theme of the theology is that Jesus has superseded the Jewish religious system. In a christological reading of the Old Testament, the author proposes that Jesus is the fulfilment of the Old Testament as High Priest (4.14—5.10; 7.1–28; 8.1—9.28). He is a pioneer and forerunner (2.10; 6.20; 12.2). The argument is driven by ideas about discipleship. The key imperatives are: hold fast (4.14; 6.18f.; 10.23), approach (4.16; 7.25; 12.22) and move on (4.11; 12.2; 13.13). The Christian life is characterized by movement. This also involves an eschatological perspective. Christians are pilgrims who are moving towards their true citizenship in heaven (11.13–16). It is this faith that motivated people in the past and it can do so in these new circumstances (11.1—12.12)

Hebrews is undoubtedly a strange book, but it does deal with a very contemporary issue – the loss of confidence, loss of interest and loss of commitment that is felt in many Christian communities.

The Bible and code

By this time the group felt quite tired, but they tried to muster enthusiasm to hear something about the book of Revelation, which held a fascination for most of them, on the grounds that to try to understand it made them feel like code-breakers or characters in a Dan Brown novel. This is an example of a book, said William, where neither historical nor social scientific approaches give us the whole story. True, there have been attempts to date the book in the mid-90s. This is said to connect well with the gruesome references to persecution in the book, which would then regard it as emerging from the persecution of Emperor Diocletian. The problem here is that actually, the only real evidence for persecution under Diocletian is the book itself. That is to say, the arguments have often been circular. Revelation could have been written any time between the late 60s of the first century AD and the second decade of the second century.

It is also true that the social situation of the seven churches addressed in chapters 2 and 3 has been well researched and documented, and there is little doubt that the situation was both known to the writer and used by him in illustration. These chapters set out an audit of seven churches in the varied area of Asia Minor, as it was then known (modern-day western Turkey). It is possible that this book gives us one of the latest assessments of church life that we find in the New Testament. For each of the churches, the author has good things to say and criticisms to make, with two exceptions. The church at Philadelphia attracts no criticism, only praise. The church at Laodicea attracts nothing but criticism. Here there is apparently nothing good to say.

William said that looking at the letter to Laodicea gave a good insight into the critical approach of the social sciences and the results of that in terms of interpretation.

TO DO

Read Revelation 3.14–22. Then listen to what William has to say. How much does this information add to your appreciation of this passage?

The town of Laodicea was famous for four things. It was a centre for healing eye ailments, based on a salve made from a local mineral spring. The lukewarm waters of that spring were also well known and, as anyone who has ever attempted to drink waters at a spa will know, they are pretty unpalatable and often induce retching. The waters of Laodicea were no exception. The town was what we would now call a banking centre – a place where Bills of Exchange could be cashed – and as surrounding towns were known for their wool and dyeing industries, Laodicea was famous for its ready-made clothing industry. The writer of Revelation writes to these people who are famous for sight, riches and clothing fashion that they are in reality poor, naked and blind. More than that, they make God retch.

In the letter to Ephesus we see anxiety about the limits of tolerance. A church that is too rigorous in setting parameters for belief, and rooting out those outside those parameters, is in danger of sacrificing the very thing that gives it identity: namely the love it is meant to exhibit (Revelation 2.4). Letters to Pergamum and Smyrna give encouragement to those who live in strongholds of the Roman imperial cult and the headquarters of other pagan religions. The letter to Thyatira fleshes out the kind of problems that Paul speaks of in 1 Corinthians in relation to food sacrificed to idols. The issue here is just how far Christians should compromise in order to engage fully with the society of which they are a part. In Thyatira, if you wanted to engage in trade you had to belong to a trade guild. If you belonged you had to eat the meals that included what seemed like tainted meat. That is the dilemma – and it is interesting that of all the churches addressed, the one in Thyatira died out first. A letter to Sardis urges the Christians against complacency. Philadelphia is a small church on the frontiers of the region. The author uses the image of working at the frontier to commend their missionary work.

Making sense of the apocalypse

William warmed to his task. Virtually every critical approach has been employed to make sense of Revelation. Some have used historical approaches to render the book rather like an *Old Moore's Almanac* of the ancient world, charting various disasters and divine interventions that will happen throughout history. Others have used a similar method to relate the message of the book entirely to its own time. Yet others have all but abandoned history and concentrated rather on the literary images of the book, relating them to the literary traditions of Old Testament apocalyptic writing and the images of books like Ezekiel in particular. What the book has to tell us about the Church is conveyed in three ways.

First the letters to the seven churches in chapters 2 and 3 do describe actual church congregations, and set out what is regarded by the author as good and bad practice within them. From these accounts we can pick out some of the threats to good order and some of the difficulties under which the churches were attempting to live and grow. There is nothing relaxed about these pictures. The author believes this to be a crucial time for them, a time of crisis.

Second, this is placed in a wider theological context, which could be said to describe what the Church is for. It is in fact part of God's plan to finalize his victory over evil. This victory was secured on the cross, but its effects are worked out over a longer timescale. Churches are the communities of the watchful and patient, being urged to refrain from idolatry and immorality so that the plan might not be frustrated.

Third, it is in the Church's worship that the seeds of victory are contained. The Church must sing its new song to thwart the powers that are ranged against it. Hence we have some indicators of what future Christian liturgy might look like. In addition to liturgical-sounding fragments and hymns we have a shape that mirrors that of the Eucharist. Chapters 4 and 5 in particular are said to reflect in turn on creation and redemption, and the whole moves towards the finale at the wedding feast of the Lamb. Some modern liturgies borrow from its language.

This was the clearest description of Revelation that Tim had heard. He looked forward to doing more reading on that basis.

Conclusion

It was time for William's finale. From Paul's genuine Letters, we were able to see the adventurous and innovative attempt to provide a theology of connectedness and unity in diversity. From the deutero-Pauline Letters and writings we can see rather more pedestrian attempts to deal with the same problem – a problem that seems to be getting worse. The response is to create authority structures, to sharpen definition of the faith in formal-sounding or creedal terms, and to close down opposition with dire threats about the eternal consequences of false doctrine. Issues around identity are clearly important, as are questions about the legitimate relations with civic powers and other belief systems. As we read these second-generation works we are acutely aware of two things. First, that much of the New Testament would not have been written were it not for some controversy raging. And second, that we have the accounts of only one side of those arguments. Here are the seeds of the issues that dominated Church discussion for the next four centuries. But it would be wrong to see all this as negative. What we see in this emerging Church are signs of real theological vitality, creative pastoral thinking and organization and a sense of being in a significant place at a significant time, and yes, a bit like the Internet social sites, with a whole set of new friends.

After he had left, the group caught its breath and exchanged views on William. He certainly gave church leaders a pasting, said Tim, what with all that stuff about internal church disputes in John, lack of inspiration in Hebrews and the dead hand of institutions in the Pastoral Letters. I still can't work out what his day job is. He's a bishop, said Ken.

Conversations with the scholars

The second volume in the SPCK Exploring the New Testament series is an excellent introduction that chimes well with, and complements, the approach in this book: Marshall, Travis and Paul (2002), *Exploring the New Testament Vol. 2: The Letters and Revelation.* On the General Letters, a good overview of current scholarly thinking is provided by Harner (2004), *What Are They Saying about the Catholic Epistles?*

On individual books, in addition to books already mentioned, a readable introduction to the Letters it names is provided by Chester and Martin (1994), *The Theology of the Letters of James*

Peter and Jude; also Donelson (2001), *From Hebrews to Revelation: A Theological Introduction.* The classic book on the Letters of John is Brown (1979), *The Community of the Beloved Disciple.* Specifically on Hebrews, a book by a great New Testament scholar is Lindars (1991), *The Theology of the Letter to the Hebrews.*

On Revelation, a well-regarded commentary which is very accessible is Sweet (1990), *Revelation* (SCM Pelican Commentaries) (2nd edn). More recently, and thinking primarily of readability, is Thompson (1998), *Revelation* (Abingdon New Testament Commentaries).

Further reading

Brown, R. E., 1979, *The Community of the Beloved Disciple*, London: Geoffrey Chapman.

Chester, A. and Martin, R. P., 1994, *The Theology of the Letters of James, Peter and Jude*, Cambridge: Cambridge University Press.

Donelson, L. R., 2001, *From Hebrews to Revelation: A Theological Introduction*, Louisville, KY: Westminster John Knox Press.

Harner, P. B., 2004, *What Are They Saying about the Catholic Epistles?*, New York: Paulist Press.

Lindars, B., 1991, *The Theology of the Letter to the Hebrews*, Cambridge: Cambridge University Press.

Marshall, H., Travis, S. and Paul, I., 2002, *Exploring the New Testament Vol. 2: The Letters and Revelation*, London: SPCK.

Sweet, J., 1990, *Revelation* (SCM Pelican Commentaries), 2nd edn, London: Penguin.

Thompson, L. L., 1998, *Revelation* (Abingdon New Testament Commentaries), Nashville, TN: Abingdon Press.

7

The Kite Runner

Fish and crosses

Ken began the session by saying that he had noticed that Alice had a badge on the bumper of her car in the shape of a fish, which was clearly a religious badge, because it had the name Jesus written within it. He invited her to tell the group what it signified. She was pleased to do so. Well basically, she said, it tells other people I'm a Christian, and she added in what was for her an astonishing piece of non-religious lateral thinking, it's a bit like having a badge with Police Federation or the Caravan Club. Why a fish? persisted Ken. Alice knew the answer to that too. There is an ancient tradition that in the early days of persecution of Christians, when the profession of allegiance could be dangerous, one secret sign that could be drawn in the sand quite easily in order to identify fellow Christians was that of a fish. Why a fish? Well, the Greek word for fish, *ichthus*, could have been a mnemonic. In the original Greek it could have included the first letters of the creedal statement, 'Jesus Christ, Son of God is saviour'. For me, she said, this is the essence of the good news and the one that is the default option for most people I know. Jesus Christ is the Son of God and saves us from our sins.

Tim remembered that when he had made his initial list he had agonized about this good news because in a sense he had thought of it as the Church's default position, setting out both the purpose of Jesus' coming (or being sent) and the reason why he died in the way he did. He had heard it in one form or another around Easter for as many years as he could remember. Jesus came to redeem us, to buy us back and to make atonement between God and God's human creation once again. And all this is to do with the cross. Abi was musing, remembering a girl she had shared a room with in college who had a big wooden cross on her bookcase. Underneath it was inscribed, 'For our sins'. It had always seemed rather stark and austere to Abi, and it was difficult to imagine such a thing being good news.

Ken went on to say that the language in which this supposed good news is expressed might sometimes seem remote and archaic, but the sentiments it describes certainly are not. The theme of two modern books (and their respective films), *Atonement* and *The Kite Runner*, is precisely our need to have the chance to make a fresh start and find a second chance. These are stories that have a huge popular appeal because we can identify with their theme.

TO DO

Ken asked if anyone had seen either film, or if they could think of other modern novels or films that had the same kind of theme. You too could join in this quest.

What Jesus did

Ken said, today I want us to unpick the claim that Jesus the redeemer made atonement for us, see what it means and what makes it good news within the New Testament itself. It will involve us in looking at how the life and work of Jesus, as set out in the New Testament, was viewed by scholars from the nineteenth century onwards. We shall look at how the gospel account of the death of Jesus, the so-called passion narrative, has been studied and the conclusions that have been reached about the relation of Jesus' life and purpose to what the Gospels contain. We shall see what other New Testament evidence there is for regarding Jesus' death on the cross for our sins as good news, or even the predominant good news. And so he began.

In the nineteenth century there was a great deal of interest in what the Gospels can tell us about the actual life of Jesus. As critical scholarship took off, there was a perceived need to separate fact, on the one hand, from commentary and interpretation on the other. The view began to emerge that what the New Testament described was the Church's faith rather than a straightforward historical account of Jesus' life and ministry. In other words, what we are reading is what faith has enabled those who reflected on events to believe about Jesus. Of course, this raised the question: how much can we know about the actual life of Jesus and, from the standpoint of the gospel, does that really matter? Alice began to look anxious.

An approach that moved away from a literal historical under-standing of the text made it possible for those with rationalist sympathies to redefine what was meant by faith. Faith did not consist necessarily in believing that incredible things had actually happened. Rather it was about trying to discern and share the faith that had compelled people to write about Jesus in a particular way. So through the nineteenth century, predominantly German scholarship effectively dismantled the supernatural elements of the Gospels, no longer holding them to be 'facts'. Miracles could be reinterpreted and other accounts that had once been regarded as straightforward description, such as the virgin birth or resurrection, could be reinterpreted in a mystical or poetic way. For some people this was a misrepresentation of the gospel, which reduced it to a series of moral exhortations and Jesus to the status of a good wise man. The idea that Jesus' death on the cross had achieved some-thing or that this had a profound bearing on how and why the Gospels were written had apparently got lost. Alice looked happier. Scholarship was apparently aware of how it had got it wrong.

Other nineteenth-century attempts to write a life of Jesus restored the supernatural perspective through the medium of eschatology. This led to a new interest in the category of Kingdom and Jesus' role in bringing it about. Was Kingdom something more than a gradual process of social improvement brought about by largely peaceful political means? This new interest had the effect of concentrating Jesus' work more on the Kingdom than on the atonement for sin.

It was only after this whole movement had run its course and the theological community had been forced to rethink all they thought they had known about Kingdom, as a result of the disillusion about human achievement following the First World War, that interest in the intention of the texts was resumed.

Fact and interpretation

The accepted wisdom was that whatever had actually happened, the New Testament as we had received it had overlaid it in a number of ways.

First, the writers had described events from the standpoint of faith. So what they described as events were in reality, it was claimed, interpretations of events. Nowadays that does not seem so scandalous. Historians and sociologists would agree that there is no such thing as an innocent text. All texts describe a point of view and have an interest. What it amounted to was a belief that the Gospels told us more about the early Church than they did about the life of Jesus.

Second, they had used the language idiom and culture of the times to describe their faith. It was argued that this 'packaging' obscured the truth to modern people rather than revealed it. So the attempt was made to strip the essential message from the medium in which it was presented and then re-present it in a new package. The term 'demythologizing' is used to describe this process. This now seems very dated, though at the time it led some to believe that the Gospels were virtually worthless as historical sources.

Third, form critics were also casting doubt on an interpretation of the Gospels as eye-witness accounts and moving towards the view that the Gospels were crafted works, using a variety of sources and combining them to produce an argument towards belief for specific contexts.

TO DO

Look at each of Ken's three points above. Which is the most challenging for you? Which the most liberating? Do you agree that all historic texts have a point of view and are 'interested' rather than 'disinterested' or neutral? What about newspaper reporting nowadays? Does that shed any light on Bible 'reporting?'

Ken continued. Clearly a key text for understanding what the basic good news was, at least as it was understood in its own time, was the Gospel of Mark. This was after all now taken to be the first Gospel, inventing the term 'gospel' and with the avowed intention of proclaiming good news. Why was that Gospel written, and what did it want to say that Jesus had achieved? Those two questions are connected. They resolve themselves into the question: if Jesus were the Messiah, why did he have to die? After all, popular expectation was that the Messiah would restore national fortune and re-establish God's rule in Jerusalem. Everything that the Gospels tell us reflects on that theme with cruel irony. What does it mean for our understanding of God to say that God has been crucified?

There is a commonly held view that the passion narrative was the first coherent form of the Gospel. There is quite a contrast in Mark's Gospel between the continuous narrative of the passion and the collection of unconnected events that precede it. Effectively, scholars have said that the first Gospel is a passion narrative with an introduction, and though Mark might be regarded as something of a pioneer in combining the two, and in collecting and editing the material that describes the typical events in Jesus' ministry, when it comes to the passion narrative he is on familiar ground. He can rely on something that was probably in existence already.

Why did Jesus die?

As an existing account it had its own rationale and theology as it
sought to answer the basic question outlined above: why did Jesus
die? A number of apologetic strands can be discerned from Mark's
text. The first essential is to portray Jesus as innocent. After all if in
the popular mind he deserved to die, no one would be persuaded
of the claims of Christianity. What gives the story its poignancy is
the depiction of innocent suffering. Here was someone who set
out to heal, teach and bring good news, but who through false
accusation was put to death prematurely. That in turn raises the
question about who was responsible. There is what appears to be
a deliberate tension between three kinds of answer. On the one
hand, sinful fallen humanity was responsible. That sinful humanity
is represented by those who had a practical hand in the events.
The practical responsibility was shared between the Jews and the
Romans. However, in the early post-Easter period it was the Jews
who were less friendly to the Church than the Romans, and there
is evidence to show that the blame for Jesus' death was more and
more directed towards them.

That having been said, there are two other answers to the question. One is that Jesus chose to die. He entered Jerusalem in the way
he did knowing what that would precipitate. Mark 10.32–45 sets
out the necessity of Jesus' death from his own lips. Beyond that, it
could be said that it was God's will that Jesus should die. We have
in the Gospel a repeated 'it is necessary' (Mark 8.3; 9.3; 10.33).
But if God had ordained that the Son of God, or Son of Man, must
suffer and die, then the contemporary faithful believed that the Old
Testament must have predicted it, because the Old Testament surely
contained the revealed will of God. Appeal to the Old Testament
provided two things. First, it helped in the apologetic task of per-
suading Jews about Jesus. Second, it gave material and a framework
for filling in the gaps of the passion story. This was the quarry from
which the theology could be mined.

But just how was that quarrying done? The answers to that
question follow the lines of the development of twentieth-century

criticism. In the earlier part of the century, the dominant thesis was that the first passion narrative grew organically from a number of sources over a period and attempts were made to try to find snapshots of the various stages of development. However, the effects of redaction criticism took the debate in a different direction from the 1960s onwards, with scholars more inclined to the view that the author of Mark had a much more central role and was completely responsible for the composition of the narrative. This view is usually held by those who see the Old Testament as being used to 'create' the story or at least give it a framework. Most recently there has been renewed interest, partly as a result of the development of literary forms of criticism, in the possibility of a fairly complete passion narrative at an early stage, which the author of Mark was able to use. This view is usually held by those who see the role of the Old Testament as offering opportunity for reflection on a narrative that is already in existence in outline. So the two possibilities are either the author of the first Gospel started with a blank piece of papyrus and imagined what might have happened using the Old Testament as a guide to what God must have intended, or the author took over a narrative that had existed (and perhaps developed) from a very early stage and used the Old Testament to offer further commentary and proof.

Alice was very unsure about this, but Ken asked everyone to look at Mark 14.32–42, then to compare it with the slightly different versions at Matthew 27.36–46 and Luke 22.39–43. First of all make sure you have noticed the differences, he said. But, he continued, if Jesus was praying alone, how could anyone have known what he was saying? They can't have overheard him because they were asleep. Someone must have assumed what he was saying. What does his prayer remind you of? What was an obvious source for this kind of material? Their answer was unanimous. Is that such a bad thing then? asked Ken.

Ken continued. Further evidence is provided for a reflective rather than a creative role for the Old Testament by a close reading of the text, which shows key elements of the story have no Old Testament pedigree. These include the fire in the courtyard at the trial, Peter's denial, the singing of a hymn after the Last Supper, the mention of Simon of Cyrene, the time scheme on the cross and the tearing of the Temple curtain.

What we are presented with, however it came into being, is an account that is both description and explanation, and the explanation responds to answer the question of why Jesus dies in terms of its being God's will. Mark's Gospel is not just a passion narrative. It has an extended introduction, which has skilfully woven the Christology of the narrative into the story of Jesus' life and ministry. The earlier part of the Gospel appears to be an answer to the question, 'Who was Jesus?' Mark's answer seems to be that Jesus' identity is most fully revealed in his suffering. Only three times in the whole Gospel is Jesus recognized as Son of God. Two of those occasions are when God does the recognizing: after the baptism (1.11) and at the transfiguration (9.7). But the third is the one that provides the real climax to the story about recognition, when Jesus is recognized as Son of God by the centurion – a Roman foreigner – after the crucifixion. This heightens rather than answers the question about why the Messiah had to die. The key text is usually identified as Mark 10.45, containing as it does not only the necessity of Jesus' death but that it also acts as 'a ransom for many'.

Jesus the suffering servant

However it is being used, the main Old Testament theme evident here is that of the suffering servant, as described most fully at Isaiah 52 and 53. Sometimes in the Synoptic Gospels there is a direct quote from that source (e.g. Isaiah 53.12 is quoted at Luke 22.37). Sometimes we hear allusions to that tradition, as in the mockery of Jesus. More generally, Jesus is portrayed as sharing characteristics with the servant. One list gives these similarities: Jesus is chosen by God to complete his mission through suffering, he willingly submits to that mission, is innocent, maintains silence, dies for many, is abused, numbered with transgressors, anticipates vindication and is vindicated after maltreatment. Although there are scholars who doubt the influence of the suffering servant theme, that is a compelling list. Some scholars believe that the words of recognition after Jesus' baptism and his transfiguration noted above are a direct echo of the introduction to the first servant song at Isaiah 42.1.

Theologically, the key thing about the Old Testament tradition is that it gives a framework for regarding suffering as redemptive. That is, it provides one answer to the age-old question of why good people should have to suffer: because it achieves something. It has to be said that the direct Gospel evidence is very slight that what is achieved is atonement for sin. There is much stronger evidence in the Gospels for the view that Jesus' death inaugurated the Kingdom and/or ushered in a new stage in history. Nevertheless, for those who want to find it, there is the definite evidence of Mark 10.45 and Matthew 26.28 that a direct link was being made between the death of Jesus, redemption and the forgiveness of sins. However, those links are made most explicit not in the Gospels but by Paul. At 1 Corinthians 15.3 he quotes a creedal statement that Christ died 'for our sins', thus bearing witness to an already current tradition just 20 or so years after the first Easter. Galatians 1.4 tells us that he 'gave himself for our sins'. Similar statements and sentiments can be found at Colossians 1.21ff.; 2.13ff.; 2 Corinthians 5.18ff. and 1 Thessalonians 5.10. It is a major theme of the Letter to the Romans.

Atonement

Ken felt he had been talking long enough about fairly difficult things and that it was time for a more general discussion linked to an activity. He asked people to split into smaller groups and think about whether suffering could be for a purpose, and how comforting that could be. The result for the group was that if you, or someone close to you, were suffering, it could seem almost cruel to say that it was for a purpose. But in retrospect, members could see how times in their lives when they had experienced suffering had actually had a positive outcome. One person even spoke of her suffering as 'a time of growth'.

TO DO

What do you think about these questions? Could suffering be
for a purpose?

Getting behind the jargon

*Traditional dogmatic theology has spent much energy on trying to work
out exactly what happened on the cross and how to describe it in a
way that is intelligible to the context of each theologian's time. This
has resulted in a number of classic theories of the atonement and since
this is such a fundamental doctrine of Christianity these theories tend
to be held very firmly by their proponents. The best known are these.
First, there is the moral influence theory. This concentrates on the love
of God and asks us to accept that God's love is beyond our imagination
but that it finds expression in this unthinkable act of crucifixion, which
should inspire believers to their own acts of grace and love. The second
is the Ransom theory and, related to it, the Christus Victor theory. Both
of these concentrate on Satan and how believers are to be freed from
his grasp, either because through his death Christ pays the ransom
to Satan and so sets the captives free, or by his death Christ defeats
Satan and so frees us from captivity to sin and death. The 'satisfaction'
theory or 'propitiation' theory is similar to that except that it is God
whose honour has to be restored after it has been degraded by human
sin. Christ's death achieves that. A development of that view, common
in evangelical hymnody, is the 'penal substitution' theory, which takes
us to the culture of the court of law. Humankind is in the dock, deserv-
edly, but Christ takes our place and vicariously is punished in our place.
He substitutes himself for us. The 'recapitulation' theory concentrates
on the literary presentation and takes its cue from the discussion in
Romans 5 and the explicit mention in 1 Corinthians 15:22 that 'as in
Adam all die, so in Christ shall all be made alive'. This theory sees Christ
as recapitulating and restoring all that Adam's disobedience destroyed.*

There can be no doubt about the centrality of the cross in the theology of Paul. He is more concerned with the death of Christ than any other New Testament writer. The genius of his theology was to begin with the cross as a fact and act of faith and then work out what new thing that was saying about God and about God's purposes for humankind. The First Letter to the Corinthians 2.2 and the preceding discussion are typical. However, many scholars believe that the long history of discussion about the theology of atonement has led to assumptions being made about Paul's contribution to the subject that are not justified. In fact, it is claimed, Paul has no one theory of the atonement. He is not concerned with the historical facts at all, but is fascinated by the principle of a crucified God, and, it is claimed, he sets out the implications of that using a number of metaphors and symbols that would appeal to different audiences. This is consistent with his overall style and method of working.

TO DO

Read 2 Corinthians 5.14—6.2 and see how many different ways Paul finds of describing what Christ did on the cross. Are you surprised at their number and variety? What does that tell you about Paul, about the New Testament generally and about this bit of good news?

Ken said, when everyone had finished, that this passage illustrates the variety of images and ideas that Paul is working with. They include reconciliation (explicitly), vicarious substitution (5.14f.), Christ as representative of all (5.14, 21), justification (5.19, 21), forgiveness (5.19), new creation, new perspective and new order (5.16f.), the love of Christ (5.14), the work of God (5.18), deliverance (6.2) and participation (5.21). This list gives some idea of how complex this area is. Just as there are many ways of presenting who Christ is, depending on the culture of the addressees, so there are many ways of presenting what Christ did and what he achieved. The key thing is that from the earliest tradition Christians believed that who Christ was and what he did were of universal significance. It was the kernel of their message.

Conclusion

Both Abi and Tim were feeling much more confident now about handling pieces of New Testament text and passing opinions about them. This particular session with its look at an area of good news surrounding Christ's identity and death had involved the group in some of the more complex areas of New Testament study, but it had certainly helped Tim reflect on his faith more fully. Abi too was making sense of the different stages of scholarship. For her, the good news is that Christianity is at heart a religion of second chances. In her head she carried the picture of kite runners running again.

Conversations with the scholars

There is a huge volume of literature on the person and work of Jesus. Key works by recognized scholars you might like to read are: Hengel (1981), *The Atonement: the Origins of the Doctrine in the New Testament*; Taylor (1982), *The Passion Narrative of St Luke: A Critical and Historical Investigation*. Otherwise the best bet is to read good Gospel commentaries on the passion narrative. Many books on this topic belong more to the area of Christian doctrine than biblical studies. One writer who writes in both disciplines is Tom Wright. See Wright (2006), *Evil and the Justice of God,* chapter 3, or, more recently and more generally, Wright (2011), *Simply Jesus.*

Further reading

Hengel, M., 1981, *The Atonement: The Origins of the Doctrine in the New Testament*, Philadelphia, PA: Fortress Press.
Taylor, V., 1982, *The Passion Narrative of St Luke: A Critical and Historical Investigation*, Cambridge: Cambridge University Press.
Wright, N. T., 2006, *Evil and the Justice of God*, London: SPCK.
Wright, N. T., 2011, *Simply Jesus*, London: SPCK.

8

Things Can Only Get Better

Good and evil

Ken was in one of his slightly scary jolly moods. Today, he said, we're going to have a music starter. The session began with the loud rendition of a song familiar to all of them: 'Things can only get better'. When eventually it had finished Ken said, I bet you're wondering why I played that. Not much gets past him, whispered Tim, and Abi began to giggle. Suddenly everyone seemed to accept it was time to get serious, as Ken went on. Perhaps the most enduring anxiety that afflicts humankind is the one that concerns good and evil. This is particularly acute for people of faith. Their faith invites them to believe that the world has been created by a benign power who wills well-being for all the creation, but their everyday experience is of injustice, war, corruption, undeserved suffering and apparently unmanaged global incompetence, not to mention natural disaster. The question is then: will God's good creation inevitably be corrupted by human evil or, on the other hand, will human evil inevitably be redeemed by God's grace? In the good and evil stakes, who's winning? The good news is that, quite simply, good wins.

This is the fundamental question posed in the Bible in the first 11 chapters of the Old Testament book of Genesis and has been described as the theme of the whole Bible. The good news that the New Testament conveys is that evil is conquered and new creation is possible. As we have seen, this is not just a theoretical issue. The writers believe that in the teachings and example of Jesus there is the opportunity for a new ethic for individuals and society that will ensure that good wins out. But in a bigger sense there is good news here. Somehow, through his death on the cross, a victory has been won by Christ, which has seen evil vanquished, even though the practical effects of all that have not quite filtered through to street level.

Ken said that in this session we would see how this theme is dealt with by two different Gospel-writers with quite different perspectives. Then we would look at Paul's approach to ethics and how he sees the cross as having changed everything. Then, finally, he said, we shall also look at the book that trumpets the victory of good over evil most dramatically, the book of Revelation.

The old covenant

Ken said it was important to start with the Old Testament. To see how Old Testament ethics developed we need to see something about the covenant relationship between God and the people of Israel.

TO DO

Read Exodus 22, or the whole of chapters 21—23, which is called the 'book of the covenant'. What are the elements of this ancient law that surprise you most? Look also at Micah 6.8.

Abi had read the whole passage and was surprised by the section 21.3–6 about slaves, which she found surprisingly humane. Tim opted for 23.12. What struck him was that Sunday was a day off for everybody, even the animals, and not just the bosses. He also liked, and was surprised by, the emphasis on hospitality to strangers and aliens. He had not realized the Old Testament was so inclusive. From what she had understood about Old Testament law, Alice was surprised that there were not far more prohibitions like the one in 22.19.

Increasingly, in later times, the Law was seen not just as an import-ant mark of cultural and ethnic identity for a dispersed people, Ken went on, but also, keeping the Law was seen as a means of hasten-ing the coming of the Messiah, the Kingdom and the new age. In other words, if human beings were good enough, God might be persuaded to intervene in human misery again. This, he went on, shows the difference between a Jewish and a Christian perspective. For Christians, God intervened when we did not deserve it and were certainly not good enough. In a sense that is the good news we were talking about in the last session. But that is one possible reason why the legalism that had invaded Judaism by the end of the Old Testament period, and that had, according to Christian accusation, robbed it of life, developed in the way it did. To flout the Law was to postpone the day when God would act. It is therefore quite natural that in New Testament times there was a strong link between ethics and eschatology. The gospel message, though, was not about what people have to do in order for God to respond. Rather the gospel message is about God's initiative and about how people have to understand what will count as law in the new Kingdom and within a new covenant, as the most famous passage in the New Testament about the new covenant (Matthew 26.28) makes clear, in the con-text of what will become the Church's defining act based on the Last Supper.

The new covenant – Matthew

The Gospel of Matthew forms the most natural bridge between Old Testament expectation and the new radical message of Jesus. Older commentators have noted that the teaching material in the Gospel is grouped into five so-called discourses, each flagged up by their concluding formulaic verse.

TO DO

The formula is: 'when Jesus had finished ...'. See if you can identify all five of these blocks of material. You will need to look for the Sermon on the Mount, the mission charge to the disciples, the parables of the Kingdom, the teaching about the Church (probably the hardest to find) and teaching about the end of the age.

At this point Ken said it would be a good idea for an activity to try to remember some of the things the group had already learned about Matthew's Gospel. They went round the room with each person contributing one thing, until they ran out of things to say. What surprised all of them was just how much they remembered. See if you can do the same. Then, he said, let's look at some things in more detail.

For example, there is a scholarly discussion about the extent of Matthew's relation to the Jews. It seems most likely that this was written to a Christian community, possibly with a majority of Jewish converts, engaged now in a controversy with Jews. Some also think that Matthew was addressing Christians who felt liberated from any law. For whatever reason, this is the Synoptic Gospel that displays most hostility to Pharisaic Judaism. Chapter 23, which is special M material, is especially vitriolic.

But, ironically, on the other hand, the Gospel could be described as the most Jewish. The fivefold structure, common within Judaism (the books of Psalms and Proverbs are divided into five, for example), was noted in the early twentieth century by B. W. Bacon, who saw the repeated, 'when Jesus had finished' (Matthew 7.28; 11.1; 13.53; 19.1; 26.1 – did you get them all?). It emerges that there are other formulae within the Gospel, which allow for different patterns to be considered (for example, as a beginning and ending 'bracket': 4.23; 9.35; or 4.17; 16.21).

The Sermon on the Mount

Matthew's eschatology has influenced the discussion about the Sermon on the Mount. Matthew is influenced by Jewish apocalyptic. He inevitably introduces or heightens apocalyptic imagery (for example at 8.12; 13.42; 22.13; 27.51–53). In keeping with apocalyptic writing this means also an emphasis on reward and punishment, which some critics believe presents a difficulty for the modern reader. Christians should not act in the hope of receiving reward or avoiding punishment. The principle of God's grace is perhaps rescued by the fact that the rewards are always greater than the deserts, and that those who are rewarded are the ones who have done what they did without thought of reward. More generally, though, there is an air of tension, redolent of apocalyptic that pervades the Gospel. Decision is required now. The time is short. Judgement is imminent. Right behaviour is a high priority. People are known by their fruit, and especially by their attitude to the least important and lowest people.

The link between this atmosphere of anxiety and ethics was seized on by Albert Schweitzer at the beginning of the twentieth century. Schweitzer believed that the demands made in the Sermon on the Mount were extreme. They could not be accommodated to normal life easily. His solution was to see them as ethics for a short time only until the Kingdom should come.

Others have also noted the extreme demands in the Sermon but reached different conclusions. They represent an ideal, perhaps, an aspiration. Or they describe the ethics of the Kingdom, which will one day be manifest but which the faithful can begin to inhabit and whose laws they can begin to practise now. Related to this discussion is the question as to whether the ethics set out here are intended as generally applicable or rather as strictly relevant only to disciples. The pressing question with regard to the way Matthew has set this up is whether we should regard Jesus as interpreting the Law of Moses or see him as a second Moses who is presenting a radically new definition of the Law.

There seemed to be a lot of questions here for something that, until now, for Abi at least, had seemed relatively straightforward. She recognized the introduction to the Sermon on the Mount, the Beatitudes, because they formed part of the service liturgy in her church sometimes, and she knew that some phrases from the Sermon had become part of everyday language, such as 'going the extra mile' or 'turning the other cheek'. But she had not really thought about how practical the new law injunctions were, or what kind of society they presupposed.

TO DO

Read Matthew 5.38–48 and think about how practical these injunctions are.

Could there be such a thing as ethics that are only relevant in one place at one time, or is goodness something that is the same at all times and places? Think about the climax to the passage in verse 48. What does that verse add to your understanding of the whole passage?

When they had finished what seemed quite a lively discussion, in which Ken was sure he heard the words 'hanging', 'scroungers' and 'war criminals', he picked up on the theme of the link with eschatology. This becomes important, he said, especially for redaction critics, when we turn to the Gospel of Luke where we find a different atmosphere. This is said to result from Luke's belief that the Church is long term, not temporary, and needs the tools and structures of establishment. There are many examples of a lessening of tension around the eschatological sayings. A comparison of, for example, Mark 9.1; Matthew 24.33 and Luke 21.30f. makes the point. A further consideration is the different audiences of the two Gospels. Luke's Gospel is addressed in the first instance to a Gentile, while Matthew's Gospel can give the impression that it is addressed to a group of anxious, driven people from a particular culture. Luke is much more measured and 'relaxed'.

Luke and ethics

We should note that between one-third and one-quarter of all Synoptic Gospel material is in Luke alone. Again Ken asked the group to share what they remembered about the distinct elements of this Gospel: either material that only occurs there or traits in the Gospel that make it recognizably different from the others. This was hugely successful. Members remembered lots of things: from the parables of the good Samaritan, the lost coin and the prodigal son to the accounts of Jesus' meeting with the ten lepers and the grateful Samaritan, his meeting with Zaccheus and the account of the walk to Emmaus. They were also able to speak about prayer, women, universalism and inclusiveness, and this gave the group confidence to deal with the text in more detail.

Ken summed up with a few additional things. Jesus' ministry as portrayed by Luke includes Samaritans, Gentiles, the poor and those despised, such as Zaccheus, who would all in their various ways be thought of as outsiders. The announcement of the ministry in the synagogue in Nazareth (4.16–21) describes a universal vision, quoting from Isaiah 61. Luke shows that he understands the rich (12.15; 16.19; 6.20f.). He includes women more obviously (7.12; 8.2f.; 10.38ff.; 23.27ff.) and has more pictures of ordinary domestic life (e.g. 7.36–50; 11.37; 11.5–8). Jesus himself is less 'emotional' than in the traditions Luke inherits (e.g. Luke 6.10, cf. Mark 3.5) and his sermon on the plain (Luke 6.20–49) contains 29 verses as opposed to Matthew's which contains 106.

The scholarly consensus is that the ethical or sermon material appeared originally in the Q source and that Luke is more faithful to it than Matthew. There are a few who believe that Luke has radically altered Matthew and effectively given a commentary on that Gospel. Almost all of Luke's material appears in Matthew. The main exception is the 'woes' that 'balance' the Beatitudes (Luke 6.24–26). The inclusion of the woes is quite consistent with Luke's overall purpose. His rehearsal of the Beatitudes is usually taken to be an expansion of, and reflection on, the passage with which he chooses to describe the opening of Jesus' public ministry from Isaiah 61 (Luke 4.18f.).

The fact that Luke includes these woes contrasts sharply the plight of the outsiders and marginalized with the lifestyle of those who live at ease. Another interesting feature is Luke including the word 'now' in four places, two in the Beatitudes and two in the woes. Also his Beatitudes and woes are all in the second person. These give an immediacy and pastoral concern that is lacking in the more formal third person in Matthew. Ken asked the group to compare this with the way the two Evangelists describe the preaching of John prior to the baptism of Jesus (Luke 3.7–14; Matthew 3.7–12). Matthew has a withering attack on the Pharisees and their assumptions of precedence. Luke has a series of practical suggestions to various categories of people in the crowds: tax collectors and soldiers, as well as ordinary folk.

What we see in these key passages is that while ethics may not be a primary concern of the Gospel-writers (in the sense that the Bible is not a handbook of ethics) it is an essential corollary of their primary good news. And that good news, in the Synoptic Gospels at least, is about the inauguration of the Kingdom, the defining characteristics of the Kingdom and the membership of the Kingdom. What each of the writers believes in these categories determines the ethical message they send out. That means that the ethical message is not isolated but forms an integral part of the good news. It is good news that Samaritans cross boundaries of suspicion. It is good news that tax collectors can decide to follow a just path. It is good news that the rich take more notice of the poverty in their midst.

Paul, faith and grace

Ken then turned to Paul's writings. We see exactly the same link between theology and ethics there, he said, but the starting point is no longer the Kingdom. For Paul it is the role of faith and grace in salvation. We might equally say that it is the role of law in salvation, for this is the nub of the argument. Paul had been brought up on a theology that said good people would be vindicated if they chose to belong to the small remnant of those who did the right thing.

This remnant would be brought to the Ancient of Days by the Son of Man (Daniel 7.13) to be vindicated for sticking to their religion and remaining faithful to God. The new element in his thinking is to see salvation not as something that humans can achieve by their own endurance or rigid adherence to the Law, but rather as something that is God's initiative and God's gift. This is becoming a bit of a repetitive theme, he said. Faith and grace are terms that are very closely related for Paul. One could almost perhaps say that, for him, grace means God's having faith in us. In any case it is an act of friendship motivated by love that invites a response.

Ken said that this was a profound point and one that the group should think more deeply about. He asked members to engage with the following activity.

TO DO

Complete one of these sentences in your own words, drawing on your own experience:

- Faith is ...
- Grace is ...

Abi chose faith, because it was easier and because her daughter was called Grace and that would have skewed her thinking. She came up with:

- Faith is believing it's possible.
- Faith is continuing despite everything.
- Faith is something I admire in other people.

She ended up with, 'Faith is loving'.

Tim opted for grace, because it looked harder. His list included:

- Grace is accepting a gift, because it makes the giver happy.
- Grace is making other people feel equal with you, even if really they are not.
- Grace is accepting other people's weakness.

He too ended up with 'Grace is loving'.

In terms of ethics and behaviour, said Ken, the response Paul's way of thinking invites is to demonstrate to others what God has demonstrated to us. In 2 Corinthians 8 and 9 we see Paul using the example of the church in Macedonia, who have organized a collection for the church in Jerusalem. The account begins with Paul writing, 'We must tell you friends, about the *grace* God has given to the churches in Macedonia.' Ken emphasized the word 'grace'. Paul goes on to describe this as 'sharing in generous service' (8.4), and compares it with God's own act of generosity in Christ (8.8). He asks for 'clear evidence of your love' (8.24) from the Corinthians. For him, generosity is a mark of having understood and taken to heart the act of God in Christ. This is far removed from a life lived under law.

What Paul is describing is two different kinds of relationship. One is the kind of relationship that involves clear boundaries and obligations, say of an employer to an employee or a landlord to a tenant. This is a formal relationship. It can be based on the fear of the weaker in relation to the stronger. It is all very third party. It has some reflections in the relation between a child and a parent. The role of the parent is to establish boundaries. The child's frequent question is, am I allowed? It is also to encourage a sense of responsibility. But when those responsibilities are fully understood, a different kind of relationship is called for. That is the kind in which laws and obligations seem quite irrelevant. This is the kind of relationship between lovers. Birthday presents are not bought out of fear or to appease but in order to bring pleasure to the other, and that is a pleasure that is ratcheted up as the other responds. Paul sees the development of religion rather like that. Law was necessary at one stage but now we have been given permission to move beyond that by God's recognition of us in Jesus. Ken said one clear statement of this was to be found at Galatians 4.1–7, and everyone read that.

From that basic theological understanding, Paul is able to respond to a number of practical concerns from churches with whom he is in contact. The Corinthian Letters give the clearest example and include 'ethical teaching' on such subjects as sexual immorality

(5.1ff.), conflict resolution (chapter 6), marital sex (7.1–7), divorce (7.10–16) and eating meat consecrated to idols (chapter 8). One writer has summed up the theme of the Letter as 'being the Church in the world'.

Codes and communities

Of particular interest throughout the Epistles, Pauline and non-Pauline, are the so-called household codes that describe appropriate behaviour for different members of a household. A good example is 1 Peter 3. An attempt is made here to connect the code with theology. As Christ was submissive before his accusers, so wives must be submissive before their husbands. Tim was a little embarrassed by this, surprisingly, more so than Abi who did not mind a little submission now and again. However, Ken said, the chief interest in this code and others like it is the choice of image. The author does not use the imagery of the law court in which we stand accused, or the marketplace where people get what they pay for. Rather, he uses the imagery of the household, which is the context for sharing and the place where gifts are received and recognized.

Ethics in the Gospel of John are also related to theology, said Ken, but in this case not directly the theology of salvation, but rather ecclesiology – John's idea of the Church. For him the community of the faithful is the focus of interest. Whereas Paul writing to the Corinthians has been summarized as 'being the Church in the world', the Gospel of John could never be described thus. For him the world is that which is opposed to the Church. The Church is characterized by its internal relations and its relationship with Christ and his relationship with the Father, as set out in the high priestly prayer in John 17 with its supplication that all may be one. Intimacy is what characterizes these relationships and so the ethical injunctions are about loving one another and serving one another, rather than loving or serving those outside the fold. The iconic example of this is the foot-washing episode at the Last Supper (John 13.1–17). This demonstrates subtly that Jesus is also the servant and obedient son of the Father, in a context of a saying that 'if I do not wash you, you will have no part in me'. It is also intimately related to the injunction at 13.34f. to love one another.

The New Testament, then, does not contain a 'stand-alone' ethic and does not present that as good news in exactly the same way as the Old Testament presents the Law. In other words, the new law is not seen in the same way as the Old Testament Law – God's gift to bring structure, identity and freedom to the people of Israel – or as a new means to salvation in itself. But in a sense New Testament ethics are all about good news: they are all about what makes the news good. These may be related to Christology, salvation, eschatology or ecclesiology, but in principle they are related to what the writer considers to be the bigger picture. This goes some way towards answering the underlying question with which we began: in the good and evil stakes, who's winning? The most explicit treatment of that theme is to be found in the book of Revelation.

Winning the war

Ken said, to be brief: essentially, this book is directed to those whose experience is at odds with their faith. Their faith tells them that Christ has won a victory over the powers of evil and ushered in the eschatological age. Their experience is of being a marginal, powerless minority overwhelmed by the evidence of the military/ economic power of the state identified as enemy/Babylon. If there has been a battle between God and the powers of this world, which seemed bent on destruction, greed, corruption, immorality, etc., then God seems to have lost. The author writes to assure this group, as they meet for worship, that there is another realm beyond the obvious, and from the perspective of that realm the war has actually been won. Hence the book consists of a strong statement of the theme of the cross/atonement, with particular vindication overtones, together with a message to endure, to resist both immorality and idolatry and to live out the promise of the future through the present in worship.

The drama of the book is heightened through its correlation with worship. As the worship reaches its climax, so does the theology. So the story starts quietly, after the letters to the seven churches in Asia, with a recital of the acts of God in creation in chapter 4. Chapter 5 rehearses the theme of redemption and has a very strong ransom theme. The Lamb, who stands for Christ, is deemed worthy, 'for you were slain and by your blood you bought for God people of every tribe and language'. The worshipping chorus pick up this theme in their hymn, 'Worthy is the Lamb who was slain' (4.9 and 12). The agenda here is a comparison with the worthiness of the audited churches. Because of the gap between faith and experience, churches and Christians are tempted towards the twin evils of idolatry and immorality. Those who resist are fêted in the images of the worship. In chapter 7 they are described as those whose robes have been washed white in the blood of the Lamb and they are the ones who shout the victory song, 'Victory to our God and to the Lamb'.

Alongside these images of purity and victory we are then shown images of evil corruption and despoliation. We are assured that God is in control of a process that will see the destruction of these things. The battle between good and evil is set in the imagery of the beast and the woman in chapter 12 as the story moves up a gear. Chapter 12 concludes with the dragon going off to wage war against 'those who keep God's commandments and maintain their witness to Jesus' (12.17). As the story moves towards its climax, the images of evil, that is, the beast and all that is suggested by the city of Babylon, are seen to lose the fight against the powers of goodness represented by the various angels, the Lamb, the Bride and the new Jerusalem.

In the final scenes Babylon is supplanted by Jerusalem. But what does Babylon stand for exactly? Are there definite equivalents for Babylon? It could be Rome. Elsewhere (e.g. 1 Peter 5.13) Babylon almost certainly means Rome. But in this context it probably means more than just one city. Rather it suggests all the power that Rome represents. Great traumatic moments tend to live on in the cultural memory. So 'holocaust' can now have a range of meanings that are not necessarily connected with Jews or extermination camps. In the area of the seven churches, the emperor cult was rife. The Romans had brought a peace to what had been a troubled area and so the citizens were often fervently loyal and very intolerant of any who chose to question anything that Rome did. The Jews in the area were well tolerated and had won a number of concessions from the Romans of which they were jealous. They had no wish to be identified with the Christians. So this was a very hostile environment for many Christians. It was an area that suffered sporadic persecution. And in a way, everything that was wrong with their world could be described by Christians as 'Babylon'. The key chapter from the point of view of practical ethics is chapter 18. Here we see what could be called the military/commercial/industrial complex that embodied so much of what was wrong – the institutionalized evil that has so many equivalents in the world of today and that some protestors see in campaigns against globalization or capitalism or the banking system – here we see all that defeated with the slogan 'Babylon the Great is fallen'.

Conclusion

For their final reflection, Ken asked the group to read Revelation 18. In modern drama and literature, he said, there was quite a lot of reference to Babylon, just as there was to the apocalypse. Now, he said, can you translate Revelation 18 into a modern setting in our world? What does Babylon mean here and now, and what would it feel like to be assured that it was fallen? And does this change your idea of what the book might be about?

The subsequent celebrations are couched in the image of a wedding feast and related closely to worship, allowing for an understanding of worship in terms of a celebration of the death of evil, even though that was not obvious everywhere. Every Eucharist could be a way of proclaiming the good news that evil is defeated. Christ is risen. Babylon is fallen. Ken finished with a flourish.

Conversations with the scholars

Recommendations have already been made with regard to the individual books of the New Testament referred to here. There are discussions to be found about the relationship of particular writers to the Law, or to other systems of ethics, especially in works on Matthew (see below). Perhaps the best thing to do is look through some books on Christian ethics and read the sections on the New Testament. One you might like to look at is Childress and Macquarrie (1986), *A New Dictionary of Christian Ethics*. A classic work on Paul's relationship to the Law is Davies (1970), *Paul and Rabbinic Judaism* (3rd edn). A recent work on New Testament ethics by a noted New Testament scholar is Burridge (2007), *Imitating Jesus: An Inclusive Approach to New Testament Ethics*.

Further reading

Burridge, R., 2007, *Imitating Jesus: An Inclusive Approach to New Testament Ethics*, Grand Rapids, MI: Eerdmans.

Childress, J. F. and Macquarrie, J. (eds), 1986, *A New Dictionary of Christian Ethics*, London: SCM Press.

Davies, W. D., 1970, *Paul and Rabbinic Judaism*, 3rd edn, London: SPCK.

9

We're Still in Business

Introduction

If the truth be told, the most immediate piece of good news for Abi (the thing that had given her the confidence and energy to take part in the Church Learning Group at all), was the fact that the Internet business she started just over a year ago looked as if it was going to succeed. Her life 18 months ago was a mess. Her husband had been made redundant. It looked as if they might lose their house. The childcare costs for their tiny toddler prohibited jobs with rigid, long hours. In desperation she found a cheap wholesale source for a particular brand of children's toy and started selling on the Internet, in a small way at first and then things really took off. Twelve months down the line she had a business that employed both her husband and herself and it is now possible to plan things from a secure base. She wondered vaguely whether New Testament writers shared the kind of emotions she had experienced and what part, if any, their writings had played in what you might call the success of Christianity. Perhaps that was too worldly a thought. Perhaps it was too prompted by a business culture that had nothing to do with the Bible or the Church. But she shared it all the same.

To her surprise, Ken took the question very seriously. He said there was certainly one New Testament writer who described the growth of the Church in a confident way, as if it was inevitable, even when it might have been faltering. That writer was the author of Luke and Acts, two books that really need to be read as one, and in fact 'we're still in business' might almost be a subtitle for Acts. Also Ken said that the relationship between the history of the early Church and Christian Scripture was an interesting area in itself and one that was not often considered. Why do we have Scriptures? Why do we consider them to be an essential part of the way we define our faith? To put it bluntly, how did the New Testament as a published whole come into being and gain its stature at all?

Tim said that while we were thinking about big questions around the concept of the New Testament as opposed to its content, how confident are we that the text of our New Testament has been handed on in a way that is trustworthy? Ken said there was more than enough for one session there, but that the questions did kind of hang together. He proposed starting by looking in Acts for descriptions of success.

What is success?

Abi offered Acts 12. This begins with an apparently hopeless situation. Herod is on a roll. He has beheaded James and now feels confident to go for Paul, so has him imprisoned, effectively awaiting death. The church prays for him and he is miraculously sprung from prison by an angel. He tells Christians what had happened. As a consequence of the escape, the guards are punished by death and then Herod gets his just deserts. The final short paragraph crowns the success of the spread of the word of God. Acts 19.8–20, Abi noticed, had a similar shape. There were some miraculous elements. The enemies of the faith were overcome, and a short paragraph summed up the continuing success.

Tim characteristically steered away from miracles and suggested Acts 6.1–7. This describes a conflict in the church along ethnic lines, with regard to the daily distribution of food. The disciples got together and agreed on a new ministry strategy. 'The whole passage reeks of good practice,' he said. Everyone agrees about everything and the work goes on. Again, immediately afterwards there is a summary of further success. Tim said this was more convincing because it showed a more mature church planning strategically and did not resort to the miraculous.

TO DO

Read the passages chosen by Tim and Abi: Acts 12; Acts 19.8–20; Acts 6.1–7. Are these passages you would have chosen? Look at the issues these readings raised for Abi and Tim. Are they the issues raised for you as well?

There were a number of issues raised for Abi and Tim by the passages they had chosen. They included:

- What exactly are we reading here? Is this history in a strict sense or is it, like the Gospels, an attempt to persuade, reading events through the eyes of faith?
- If it is the latter, what is the story we are being asked to accept?
- What is the relationship between this account and the Gospels? Does this give us new information about Jesus or God?
- All of the passages describe the exercise of power in some way. What are we to make of this?
- For whom was this good news originally?

What kind of book is Acts?

The question about the genre of Acts is one scholarly area of interest. What we are presented with is a continuous narrative that has a clear agenda, namely to show that the growth of the Church was God-ordained and inevitable. Its growth is described in very idealistic terms from the foundations of the Twelve, reconstituted after the death of Judas, through the Jewish network via Peter, and then to the wider Gentile world via Paul. Its climax is the arrival of Paul at Rome, effectively the capital of the world. However, the style is not that of an academic historian. There are amusing interludes. For example, in Acts 12.13ff., Peter comes to the door of the house of John Mark's mother where the disciples are meeting. There is a very detailed description of a comic episode in which the maid who answers the door to Peter is so overcome that she shuts it again in his face, and he has to keep on knocking. There are also some very swashbuckling adventures, described in great detail as, for example, in chapter 27, and extended courtroom dramas, as in chapters 24–26. In those respects it is reminiscent of the Gospels. So perhaps it is best to read this as we might read a Gospel, accepting some basis in history and tradition but making allowance for the agenda and faith standpoint of the author.

Questions about the purpose of the book have also found different answers. Some scholars have thought that the purpose was externally driven, as it claims to be, presenting the Christian faith to a non-Christian audience. Perhaps it was even intended to persuade the Roman Empire that Christianity should be recognized officially. The counter argument is that if that was its prime purpose it is fairly unconvincing, since it demands familiarity and sympathy with a fair amount of relatively inaccessible theology. Another view is that it is a piece of polemical argument against Gnostic sympathizers, stressing the apostles as the guarantors of the faith and playing down the titles 'Christ' and 'Christ Jesus' in favour of simply 'Jesus'. Others have seen an evangelistic role for the book, seizing on passages such as 13.1–12; 16.25–34 and 26.24–29 to argue that the aim is to convert the Roman world. Others, noting the frequent references to property, have seen its evangelistic focus as being the rich and seen a link between that purpose and a secondary purpose of the Gospel of Luke.

TO DO

Read Acts 13.1–12; 16.25–34; 26.24–29. These are sometimes called as evidence for an evangelistic role for the book. Are you convinced?

Among 'internal' solutions is the popular nineteenth-century attempt to see the book as trying to reconcile the Petrine Jewish and the Pauline Gentile sections of the Church. In the mid-twentieth century the suggestion that the book formed part of an elaborate theological scheme was explored. This was associated with what was described as 'salvation history', an attempt, before the rise of literary approaches to the New Testament, to find a way of reconciling the account in the Gospels and Acts with actual history. The result was to see two ways of describing time and events. One would be recognizable to academic historians, with a linear timescale giving the ability to chart development. The other, so-called salvation history, was to divide the history of the world into epochs, based on significant events within them, from the standpoint of faith. So we might talk about the time of the prophets, the time of Jesus and the time of the Church. In this scheme, it was claimed that Acts would have described the third of these. Others, again taking a serious theological stance, have seen Acts as presenting theological development in thinking about salvation itself.

Perhaps the most convincing theory is that the book was addressed to believers to strengthen and encourage them, by demonstrating that God is in control of history and that they will in the end be vindicated for their faith. If this sounds familiar as the engine behind apocalyptic writing, then that is what you might expect when both sets of writers are concerned with a theology of history. The main difference, though, is that Acts is not written in the context of the expectation of an imminent new intervention by God. The ascension, rather than the parousia, is the key event for Luke. The Church itself is the new community of God. God's presence within it is what provides it with power.

That presence is described first of all in terms of the Holy Spirit. The term 'Holy Spirit' occurs five times in Matthew and four in Mark but 53 times in Luke and Acts. The name of Jesus is also powerful to heal and forgive (as at Acts 3.6f.). Acts 2.21 and 4.12 are very powerful statements of the power of Jesus' name. The third aspect of the presence of God is the preaching of the word. In Acts 12.24 and 19.20, for example, it is the power of the word that is associated with the success claimed. The final way in which God is present is in the lives of the followers who seek to continue his ministry in theirs. All of this has a very modern feel and if we were to add the Emmaus experience of recognizing the presence of Jesus in the breaking of the bread we would have effectively the basis of any modern account of the presence of God.

In so far as this is a book about the Church, it has a particular view of the Church. This is quite important, since a naive reading of the New Testament might suggest that there was only one view of what the Church was and how it should be ordered, and that Acts was the definitive history of that. In fact there are various views and a variety of practice, of which Luke's descriptions are one contribution to what was obviously a lively debate. The key theme for him is nevertheless a mature and inclusive one, although some writers have noted how women, who played such a large part in the Gospel, appear to have faded from sight somewhat by the time we get to Acts. Overall the theme could be summed up as unity in diversity. The apostles have a key part in guaranteeing its integrity, but there are early moves away from a rigid hierarchical model in the direction of pragmatism. Ministry to Gentiles is a key element, as are the issues of growth and success noted earlier. A mark of the presence of God is fellowship. The Church exists for a definite mission. It has to do, not just be.

One of the activities for the week was one that identified exactly with Abi's interest. The task was to imagine that the Church was a person and then to sketch a short biography, as members of the group imagined Luke might have written it. The other appealed more to Tim: imagine Luke writing a business plan for the Church. What might it have looked like? Abi was disappointed in a vague kind of way, hearing the responses, that so many of the group had called their church 'Mary'.

How has Acts reached us today?

Both Abi and Tim were surprised when Ken began the next session by saying that in one ancient manuscript (which he referred to as 'D') the text of the Acts of the Apostles was 10 per cent longer than in the versions most people read in English. He asked what kinds of question this raised for the group. Abi immediately wondered what she'd been prevented from reading and what difference it might have made. She also wondered how such a thing could have happened. Tim wondered who decided what version of the text was correct or authentic and on what grounds they did so. Both were interested to know more about how the text had been handed on through the generations. Ken began by describing the different forms in which the text of the New Testament was found.

The earliest kind of ancient book was the scroll. These were made from the leaves of the papyrus plant (Job 8.11 refers to this). The Dead Sea Scrolls are a collection of papyri. Amazingly there are papyri containing bits of the New Testament that can be dated back to the second century AD. All the papyri are classified by being given a 'p' number. So p46, dating from around the year 200, contains ten epistles of Paul. The papyrus p52, a very ancient papyrus from the first half of the second century, has just a few verses from the Gospel of John. There is reference in the Gospels themselves to the use of scrolls (e.g. Luke 4.17), but they were unwieldy to use and impossible to cross reference, as well as being awkward to store.

And so the codex appeared as a development in the early second century. This is the kind of leaf book with which we are all familiar today, but rather than being written on paper, which was unknown in the region at that time, it was written on parchment: skins of animals shaved and dressed with chalk. The name comes from Pergamum in modern-day Turkey where the new process was developed. Codexes allowed the binding of several works into one text, which made possible cross reference and meant that you could write on both sides of the page.

TO DO

What do you think are the strengths and limitations of writing with scrolls? How many references to scrolls can you find in the New Testament, and what do the results tell you about how Scripture was handed on?

Uncials and minuscules

Book script was in capital letters – so-called uncials – rather than cursive handwriting script. It was not until the ninth century that a form of cursive script was used. These later codex manuscripts are called minuscules to distinguish them from the earlier uncials. Some of the most famous and most reliable texts are uncials. One, discovered at St Catherine's Monastery on Mount Sinai by a German traveller in 1844 and called Sinaiticus as a result, is the only complete uncial New Testament. Others from the early centuries include Vaticanus, a mid-fourth-century uncial containing all the New Testament apart from a short portion of Hebrews, and Bezae, named after its discoverer in 1581, which contains the four Gospels, Acts and 3 John. This fifth- or sixth-century text is now in Cambridge.

With the ninth-century 'explosion' of minuscules, far more book versions of the New Testament were available, but they were not the only sources of information. Another important source was the very early translations of the New Testament into languages other than the original Greek. A translation into Syriac in the fifth century, called the Peshitta, exists in quite large quantities. The translation into Latin by St Jerome at the end of the fourth century, called the Vulgate, exists in over 8,000 manuscripts.

The translation history of the New Testament is a stirring story in itself. In many cases alphabets were developed so that a written text could be produced in languages that, until then, had had only spoken forms. Such was the case with Gothic, Armenian and Georgian (interestingly thought to be a language not related to any other). Another source was ancient writings from the early Church Fathers when they quoted the New Testament, and there were some copies of ancient lectionaries, which included the readings in the way some modern prayer or service books do in churches today. With all these potential sources, how do you choose which version is correct?

Ken explained that the key was to understand how variations occurred in the first place. He said you had to imagine scribes working away in dim light, perhaps copying or perhaps taking a kind of dictation. So some changes were due to faulty eyesight and some to faulty hearing. The word in Greek for 'washed' and the word for 'freed' sound identical. So at Revelation 1.5, some manuscripts have the one reading and others the other. Other changes are easy to imagine: missing a line out, thinking you remember the line but actually remembering something very similar to it from a completely different place, incorporating marginal notes into the text.

Of more importance, though, are the intentional changes made when scribes think they know better than the text in front of them. Most insidious are doctrinal alterations, often very difficult to spot. The trick for the modern scholar is to choose the reading that best explains the origin of the others. That might mean reference to things like geographical origins, relation of texts to each other and date. But there is a more subtle and subjective task, which is guided by a number of accepted principles. For example, if you have two alternatives and one makes perfect sense and the other is barely intelligible, which do you choose as the original? The answer is the second. You can understand why someone might change a text to make it make sense. You cannot understand why someone should alter sense to make it gibberish. An example is Hebrews 2.9. Some witnesses read '[Jesus] suffered death, so that by the grace of God he should experience death for all mankind'. Others substitute 'by the grace of God' with 'without God', the phrases in Greek being quite similar. It is easier to imagine why someone might change the potentially scandalous 'without God', to the more acceptable 'by the grace of God'. It is much harder to see how this could have happened the other way round. Ken said this was a much bigger subject than he had time to deal with, but as an exercise he asked everyone to look in their Bibles at the ending of the Gospel of Mark.

> **TO DO**
>
> Follow Ken's advice and explore the ending of Mark's Gospel. Compare as many English versions as you can get hold of. Look at the different possibilities and see if you can tell the story of how this text 'developed'.

Here there was not just a word or two difference, but a huge difference, and apparently four different options for an authentic text. One version ends at 16.8 with the words 'and they were afraid'. A second rounds off that verse with a final flourish, ending with the words 'the imperishable message of eternal salvation'. The third, the one that appears in the Authorised or King James Version, contains verses 9–14, and then there is an expanded version of that which concludes at verse 20. Ken asked, bearing in mind what we've heard, which text would you choose? He pointed out that there is a huge change of style between verses 8 and 9, and that the longer versions contain 17 words found nowhere else in Mark. The second alternative is very 'smooth', and the short ending is the one that has the earliest attestation. That leaves a further question. If this is the correct ending, why did Mark finish his Gospel like that?

Establishing the canon

Abi was surprised at how interesting she had found a session she had not expected to enjoy very much. Tim felt his appetite had been whetted for the other outstanding issue: the question of how the New Testament itself came into being. Ken described this subject under the heading 'canon'. This word originally described a standard measure. A modern equivalent might be 'yardstick'.

There were two things that surprised both Tim and Abi from the outset. The first was that the final canon, the contents of the New Testament as we now have it, was not fixed until 367, hundreds of years after the New Testament period. The other was that there were apparently very many pieces of religious writing produced by the early Church and its heretical offshoots, some of them written around the same time as some of the books that made it into the canon. The issue was one of choosing what should be in and what should be out. Neither Tim nor Abi had ever imagined such a thing taking place. As an initial exercise Ken asked the group to list the kind of criteria they thought might have been employed by some early church committee to decide on whether books should be included in the New Testament or not.

TO DO

Join Abi and Tim in their exercise. What do you think quali-fied a book to be in the New Testament? Or what might have counted as a disqualification? If you were recommending a book about Christianity to a non-Christian friend, how would you choose it?

Tim thought that being 'on message' was probably important. Others were shocked by this. This might have meant that only one party view was included or given preference. Tim thought that was inevitable in a situation where there were many interpretations of the truth and some people had power to decide. Abi thought that over a period of time some texts would just have fallen into regu-lar use. On her list also was 'it depends who wrote it'. Something written by an apostle would surely have a better chance than some much later work by an unknown. Ken said that from the way the history of the formation of the canon developed, all of those were important elements: apostolic authorship, orthodoxy, antiquity and use in church services.

We have to remember that in New Testament times the canon of the Old Testament had not even been fixed. Two parts of it had – the Law and the Prophets – but the third part, the Writings (includ-ing books like Job, Psalms and Chronicles), was not fixed until the very end of the first century AD. Nevertheless the concept of canon was part of the Jewish inheritance and useful when the apostles began to die and their living testimony, and the authority it carried, was lost. What is perhaps the latest book of the New Testament, 2 Peter, contains the first reference to something like a canon at 3.16. Other early church writers from around the turn of the first century appear to quote from Paul and 1 Peter, suggesting that their works had been collected or were familiar and in use. Around 150, Justin Martyr, describing an early Eucharist service speaks of reading from 'the Memoirs of the Apostles'. Around 140, someone dubbed a heretic, Marcion, published his own canon and that probably spurred the Church to think about an orthodox alternative. The second and third centuries saw a developing consensus.

Some books were never in doubt, and they include most of our New Testament. The most controversial were Hebrews, 2 and 3 John, 2 Peter, James and Jude. Writings that were accepted by parts of the Church for different periods but that did not make the final cut included *The Shepherd of Hermas*, *1 Clement*, the *Apocalypse of Peter* and the *Epistle to Barnabas*. Many of these can be read in a modern collection entitled 'The Apostolic Fathers'.

Both Tim and Abi were left with food for thought by learning more about the canon. They have come to see that searching for 'norms' is no longer thought appropriate in New Testament study and that all the talk is of unity in diversity, loose coalitions of churches rather than one unified monolith, and healthy debate among competing factions. They realize that modern study is sceptical about apostolic authorship for any of the books of the New Testament. They accept that the distinction between Scripture and tradition has broken down, and all of this is prompting them to think again about what inspiration means and how best to describe this most famous and influential of all collections of writings that we call the New Testament.

In their final activity, Ken said that some scholars regarded some books of the New Testament as more valuable than others – even wanting to ditch some altogether. The final task was to see if the group thought that there really is any 'useless' book that the collection could lose and if from our own generation there is any work of

Christian profundity that could take its place. What would that tell us about how we view the New Testament today?

Conclusion

This session has followed a thought stimulated by Abi's piece of good news, 'We're still in business'. Abi's good news began a conversation with the author of two books of the New Testament that work together to tell one connected story: Luke's Gospel and the Acts of the Apostles. The good news of Acts is that the work God began in Jesus is still continuing and thriving.

Exploring the good news of Acts has prompted us to examine some fundamental questions addressed by New Testament scholars: questions like what kind of book is Acts, how Acts and indeed the other books have reached us today, and about how we make the right choices between different ancient text versions. There are questions also about how the canon of the New Testament was settled in the fourth century and, most importantly of all, about how conversation is established between our experiences of life and the word of God in the Bible.

Conversations with the scholars

Books you might like to read on Acts include Cadbury (1958), *The Making of Luke-Acts*. This is a landmark study that established the link between the two books and effectively resolved that issue. Also, you could read Esler (1987), *Community and Gospel in Luke-Acts*. A good commentary is Scott Spencer (1997), *Acts* (New Bible Commentaries). You will find a wider discussion of contemporary issues in Powell (1991), *What Are They Saying about Acts?*

On both the text of the New Testament and its canon, the key author is Bruce Metzger. See Metzger (1987), *The Canon of the New Testament: Its Origin, Development and Significance.*

Further reading

Cadbury, H. J., 1958, *The Making of Luke-Acts*, London: SPCK.

Esler, P., 1987, *Community and Gospel in Luke-Acts*, Cambridge: Cambridge University Press.

Metzger, B. M., 1987, *The Canon of the New Testament: Its Origin, Development and Significance*, Oxford: Clarendon Press.

Powell, M. A., 1991, *What Are They Saying about Acts?*, New York: Paulist Press.

Scott Spencer, F., 1997, *Acts* (New Bible Commentaries), Sheffield: Sheffield Academic Press.

10

Bring and Share

The group's final session was billed more as a social event than a seminar. It was to be a bring and share supper with an opportunity to reflect critically on the course and share what individuals had got out of it. In preparation, and so they would not be the only ones tongue-tied and looking silly, both Abi and Tim had made some lists and notes of their own in preparation for the session. Actually most other people had too.

Tim had come to learn more and to equip himself to make a more intelligent contribution to debate (or indeed, just conversation) about Christianity, and the New Testament in particular. He had wanted to move away from a presentation of religion that relied on what were for him relatively meaningless slogans or trite clichés and to see if there was anything more. He had been well satisfied with the course. It had assured him that there was a rational academic integrity to the study of the Bible that was not at odds with faith, and it had given him lots of fresh insights and leads that he was looking forward to following as he read and heard the Bible in future.

Abi had seen the course as a kind of duty she could perform to show God she was still interested. She might not have phrased it like that, but rather in terms of finding new things about the faith she professed that would give fresh impetus to her wanting to be more involved. She too was more than satisfied. Of particular value to her was the underlying assumption that for something to be good news it has to be good news in our experience, and she had really valued the search for links between the texts' ancient meanings and their applications for today. Along the way she had learned more than she expected about the New Testament and been surprised by how little she knew about it, when she had assumed she was fairly familiar.

Alice was glad she had come. She was the kind of person who always felt happiest in a church group of any kind, but there were times when her own assumptions had been challenged and she felt that she was not quite the same person who had started the course.

Ken set out what the group had covered. He said, although we set about it in what some people might think of as rather a strange way, we have dealt with the main introductory critical questions about the Gospels. We have looked at each in some detail and seen their distinctive traits. We have spent some time on Acts and engaged with the life of the early Christian communities through the Letters, both from Paul and from other writers, and have been introduced to some of the critical issues surrounding them. We have had an introduction to the Apocalypse. We have unpacked some of the technical jargon and followed some important critical debates. We have grappled with the message and theology of the New Testament (or perhaps I should say messages and theologies), looking at important concepts such as what Jesus' death on the cross really meant, or why the Bible is interested in the end of the age. Hopefully we've excited some interest in the adventure of theology.

In the discussion that followed everyone took part. Ken took down the main conclusions on a flipchart. What do you feel you can do now, that you could not do before you came? he had asked. His chart filled with answers, such as:

- I feel that I know my way round the New Testament now.
- I can recognize the differences of style and content between the different Gospels.
- I feel able to cross-reference passages from the Synoptic Gospels and to enjoy working out why they are different.
- I feel more confident to read books that I had never read before, such as the Pastoral Letters.
- I would feel able to read other scholarly books about the New Testament and feel confident that it would not all be over my head.

- I can place the developments in the story of the early Christians, and I find that fascinating.
- I feel I have new permission to have my own view on things and new confidence to work it out.

> **TO DO**
>
> Can you identify with any of these? What might you add from your experience of your course?

'One thing I've discovered from the very first week,' said a rather more confident Alice. They all waited. 'I've discovered I like curry,' she said.

References

Achtemeier, P., 1996, *1 Peter* (Hermeneia Commentaries), Minneapolis, MN: Fortress Press.

Barton, J. (ed.), 1998, *The Cambridge Companion to Biblical Interpretation*, Cambridge: Cambridge University Press.

Bornkamm, G., Barth, G. and Held, H. J., 1963, *Tradition and Interpretation in Matthew*, London: SCM Press.

Boxall, I., 2007, *SCM Studyguide: The Books of the New Testament*, London: SCM Press.

Brown, R. E., 1979, *The Community of the Beloved Disciple*, London: Geoffrey Chapman.

Brown, R. E., 1988, *The Gospel and Epistles of John: A Concise Commentary*, Collegeville, MN: The Liturgical Press.

Burkett, D., 1999, *The Son of Man Debate: A History and Evaluation*, Cambridge: Cambridge University Press.

Burkett, D., 2002, *An Introduction to the New Testament and the Origins of Christianity*, Cambridge: Cambridge University Press.

Burridge, R., 2007, *Imitating Jesus: An Inclusive Approach to New Testament Ethics*, Grand Rapids, MI: Eerdmans.

Cadbury, H. J., 1958, *The Making of Luke-Acts*, London: SPCK.

Carter, W., 2006, *John: Storyteller, Interpreter, Evangelist*, Peabody, MA: Hendrickson.

Chester, A. and Martin, R. P., 1994, *The Theology of the Letters of James, Peter and Jude*, Cambridge: Cambridge University Press.

Childress, J. F. and Macquarrie, J. (eds), 1986, *A New Dictionary of Christian Ethics*, London: SCM Press.

Davies, W. D., 1970, *Paul and Rabbinic Judaism*, 3rd edn, London: SPCK.

Dodd, C. H., 1961, *The Parables of the Kingdom*, rev. edn, London: Collins.

Donelson, L. R., 2001, *From Hebrews to Revelation: A Theological Introduction*, Louisville, KY: Westminster John Knox Press.

Dunn, J. D. G., 1995, *1 Corinthians*, Sheffield: Sheffield Academic Press.

Dunn, J. D. G. (ed.) (2003), *The Cambridge Companion to Saint Paul*, Cambridge: Cambridge University Press.

Elliott, J. H., 1990, *A Home for the Homeless*, 2nd edn, Minneapolis, MN: Fortress Press.

Elliott, J. H., 1993, *What is Social Scientific Criticism?*, Minneapolis, MN: Fortress Press.

Esler, P., 1987, *Community and Gospel in Luke-Acts*, Cambridge: Cambridge University Press.

Fuller, R. H., 1969, *The Foundations of New Testament Christology*, London: Collins.

Gowan, D. E., 2000, *Eschatology in the Old Testament*, 2nd edn, Edinburgh: T. and T. Clark.

Gowler, D. B., 2000, *What Are They Saying about the Parables?*, New York: Paulist Press.

Green, J. B., McKnight, S. and Marshall, I. H. (eds), 1992, *Dictionary of Jesus and the Gospels*, Leicester: InterVarsity Press.

Harner, P. B., 2004, *What Are They Saying about the Catholic Epistles?*, New York: Paulist Press.

Hawthorne, G. F., Martin, R. P. and Reid, D. G., 1993, *Dictionary of Paul and His Letters*, Leicester: InterVarsity Press.

Hengel, M., 1981, *The Atonement: The Origins of the Doctrine in the New Testament*, Philadelphia, PA: Fortress Press.

Hooker, M. D., 1979, *Studying the New Testament*, London: Epworth Press.

Horrell, D. G., 2006, *An Introduction to the Study of Paul*, 2nd edn, London: T. & T. Clark.

John, J., 2001, *The Meaning in the Miracles*, Norwich: Canterbury Press.

Lindars, B., 1991, *The Theology of the Letter to the Hebrews*, Cambridge: Cambridge University Press.

Marsh, J., 1968, *Saint John: The Pelican Gospel Commentaries*, London: Penguin Books.

Marshall, H., Travis, S. and Paul, I., 2002, *Exploring the New Testament Vol. 2: The Letters and Revelation*, London: SPCK.

Meeks, W., 1983, *The First Urban Christians*, New Haven, CT: Yale University Press.

Metzger, B. M., 1987, *The Canon of the New Testament: Its Origin, Development and Significance*, Oxford: Clarendon Press.

Moule, C. F. D., 1981, *The Birth of the New Testament*, 3rd edn, London: A. and C. Black.

Perrin, N., 1963, *The Kingdom of God in the Teaching of Jesus*, London: SCM Press.

Powell, M. A., 1991, *What Are They Saying about Acts?*, New York: Paulist Press.

Powell, M. A., 1993, *What is Narrative Criticism?*, London: SPCK.

Powell, M. A. (ed.), 1999, *The New Testament Today*, Louisville, KY: Westminster John Knox Press.

Richards, H. J., 1973, *The First Christmas: What Really Happened?*, London: Collins.

Richards, H. J., 1975, *The Miracles of Jesus: What Really Happened?*, London: Collins.

Robinson, J. A. T., 1957, *Jesus and His Coming*, London: SCM Press.

Russell, D. S., 1992, *Divine Disclosure*, London: SCM Press.

Schweizer, E., 1961, *Church Order in the New Testament*, London: SCM Press.

Scott Spencer, F., 1997, *Acts* (New Bible Commentaries), Sheffield: Sheffield Academic Press.

Stambaugh, J. and Balch, D., 1986, *The Social World of the First Christians*, London: SPCK.

Sweet, J., 1990, *Revelation* (SCM Pelican Commentaries), 2nd edn, London: Penguin.

Taylor, V., 1982, *The Passion Narrative of St Luke: A Critical and Historical Investigation*, Cambridge: Cambridge University Press.

Theissen, G., 1982, *The Social Setting of Pauline Christianity*, Edinburgh: T. and T. Clark.

Thompson, L. L., 1998, *Revelation* (Abingdon New Testament Commentaries), Nashville, TN: Abingdon Press.

Trocmé, E., 1997, *The Childhood of Christianity*, London: SCM Press.

Wenham, D. and Walton, S., 2001, *Exploring the New Testament, Vol. 1, Introducing the Gospels and Acts*, London: SPCK.

Wright, N. T., 1997, *What St Paul Really Said*, New York: Eerdmans.

Wright, N. T., 2006, *Evil and the Justice of God*, London: SPCK.

Wright, N. T., 2011, *Simply Jesus*, London: SPCK.